"Krieger's voice is authentic, h⟨ own extensive experience with the voices of trans people and other clinicians to create an informative, easy-to-digest manual appropriate for both new and seasoned therapists."
—*Laura Erickson-Schroth, MD, MA, LGBTQ psychiatrist and writer of* Trans Bodies Trans Selves *and* "You're in the Wrong Bathroom!" and 20 Other Myths and Misconceptions About Transgender and Gender Nonconforming People

"A remarkably comprehensive and useful book for therapists as well as parents and people who want to learn more about gender diversity and options for transition. Irwin Krieger is an experienced clinician and a great teacher; he has the ability to take complex issues and make them simple and easy to understand."
—*Katherine (Kit) Rachlin, PhD, clinical psychologist and senior gender specialist, New York and co-author of* Standards of Care for the Health of Transgender, Transsexual, and Gender Nonconforming People V.7, *2011*

"This book is an absolute must-read for counselors who work with youth. Irwin's inviting style combined with his clinical acumen result in a fantastic and much-needed guide for working with trans and non-binary youth, a frequently misunderstood group."
—*Colt Keo-Meier, PhD, Licensed Psychologist specializing in gender and sexuality*

"Given the growing interest in gender affirmative care for trans and non-binary teens, Irwin Krieger's book arrives right on time. It capably fills a wide gap in the literature for professionals who want to support ethical clinical care for youth and their families."
—*Rachel Pepper, LMFT, author of* Transitions of the Heart

of related interest

Are You a Boy or Are You a Girl?
Sarah Savage and Fox Fisher
Illustrated by Fox Fisher
ISBN 978 1 78592 267 1
eISBN 978 1 78450 556 1

The Voice Book for Trans and Non-Binary People
A Practical Guide to Creating and Sustaining
Authentic Voice and Communication
Matthew Mills and Gillie Stoneham
ISBN 978 1 78592 128 5
eISBN 978 1 78450 394 9

Transitioning Together
One Couple's Journey of Gender and Identity Discovery
Wenn B. Lawson and Beatrice M. Lawson
ISBN 978 1 78592 103 2
eISBN 978 1 78450 365 9

Trans Voices
Becoming Who You Are
Declan Henry
Foreword by Professor Stephen Whittle, OBE
Afterword by Jane Fae
ISBN 978 1 78592 240 4
eISBN 978 1 78450 520 2

Can I tell you about Gender Diversity?
A guide for friends, family and professionals
CJ Atkinson
Illustrated by Olly Pike
ISBN 978 1 78592 105 6
eISBN 978 1 78450 367 3
Part of the Can I tell about...? Series

Who Are You?
The Kid's Guide to Gender Identity
Brook Pessin-Whedbee
Illustrated by Naomi Bardoff
ISBN 978 1 78592 728 7
eISBN 978 1 78450 580 6

Counseling Transgender and Non-Binary Youth

THE ESSENTIAL GUIDE

Irwin Krieger

Jessica Kingsley *Publishers*
London and Philadelphia

First published in 2017
by Jessica Kingsley Publishers
73 Collier Street
London N1 9BE, UK
and
400 Market Street, Suite 400
Philadelphia, PA 19106, USA

www.jkp.com

Library of Congress Cataloging in Publication Data
A CIP catalog record for this book is available from the Library of Congress

British Library Cataloguing in Publication Data
A CIP catalogue record for this book is available from the British Library

ISBN 978 1 78592 743 0
eISBN 978 1 78450 482 3

Printed and bound in the United States

To John, Ezra and Rosie

Contents

About the Author

Irwin Krieger, LCSW, is a clinical social worker in Connecticut who has provided psychotherapy for Lesbian, Gay, Bisexual and Transgender (LGBT) individuals, couples and families for over 30 years. In addition to working in private practice, he was on the mental health team at AIDS Project New Haven from 2004 to 2015. He was a 2013 recipient of the New Haven Pride Center's Dorothy Award for his service to the LGBT community in New Haven.

Since 2004, Irwin has worked extensively with transgender teens and adults and their families, as a therapist and a clinical supervisor. With the goal of expanding the base of knowledgeable providers for transgender individuals, Irwin provides training and consultancy for mental health and health care professionals, as well as school personnel. He has presented at the World Professional Association for Transgender Health Symposium in Atlanta, the Philadelphia Trans Health Conference, Boston Children's Hospital, the Maine Academy of Family Physicians, Yale University and the University of Connecticut. From 2012 to 2016 he was a consultant for the Transgender Care Team at Yale Health Plan. Irwin Krieger is the author of *Helping Your Transgender Teen: A Guide for Parents*.

For more information on Irwin and his work, visit www.IKriegerTraining.com.

Acknowledgments

Thanks to Bobbi Mark for your enthusiastic support and guidance, and to Amanda Mecke for believing I had a valuable book to offer and teaching me how to write a book proposal.

Maria Tupper, Amy Myers, Vincent Samuolis, Alan Krieger, Marguerite Ruppenicker and Lynette Adams read and commented on various chapters of this book. John Mayer reviewed and offered suggestions on every chapter. Thanks to all of you for your valuable input.

Thanks to my early teachers about trans identities: Randi Ettner, Lois Spivack, Edgardo Menvielle and Norman Spack; and to the generous World Professional Association for Transgender Health (WPATH) members who gave their time and insights when I called on them.

It has been a pleasure to collaborate with my dedicated colleagues in transgender care in New England. Among them, Robin McHaelen, Robina Altbrandt, Ilja Hulinsky, Tony Ferraiolo and the Boston Children's Hospital Gender Management Service (GeMS) Conference crew have been especially important to my development as a clinician for transgender youth.

Thanks to Andrew James at Jessica Kingsley Publishers, for seeking me out, for your enthusiasm about this book and for your editorial input. Thanks, also, to Alexandra Holmes, Yojaira Cordero,

Hannah Snetsinger, Emily Badger and the staff at Jessica Kingsley Publishers for your help. I greatly appreciate the prompt and thoughtful responses I have received at every step in this process.

To my children, Rosie and Ezra, thanks for your interest in my work on this project. I'm proud of you both for what you have accomplished so far, and excited to see what the future brings. To my partner, John Mayer, immense thanks for your patience and support while I was immersed in writing this book.

Thanks to all of the clinicians who have sought me out for supervision in your work with transgender youth. I have learned as much from you as I hope you have learned from me. And a special thanks to all of the youth and families who shared your stories and your struggles with me.

INTRODUCTION

CHAPTER 1

What a Difference a Decade Makes

Rapid Change in the Lives of Transgender Youth

In 2004 I began receiving referrals of transgender youth from True Colors, a wonderful organization in Connecticut that serves Lesbian, Gay, Bisexual and Transgender (LGBT) youth. At the time I was a clinical social worker in private practice in New Haven. For many years my psychotherapy practice had been focused on serving the LGBT community of greater New Haven. Many of my clients were gay or lesbian, few were bisexual or transgender; and the few transgender individuals I had helped were middle-aged or older. These new younger clients inspired me with their determination to be their true selves under very difficult circumstances. I admired their parents, who struggled with tremendous fears and concerns about making reasonable and safe decisions at this challenging juncture. I learned as much as I could about transgender identity, the lives of transgender people, and the professionals in my area and elsewhere who were trying to help them in their journeys toward full authenticity.

In the years since then I have worked with over 200 transgender clients. About half were 21 years old or younger. I have also supervised other therapists working with transgender youth. This book is a guide for those of you who are caring for transgender teens and young adults. Things have changed a lot for transgender youth in the United States since 2004. We have seen the emergence of publicly recognized transgender individuals including Chaz Bono, Laverne Cox, Jazz Jennings and Caitlyn Jenner. The feature film *Transamerica* came out in 2005 with little notice, while *Transparent* premiered on Amazon in 2014 to great acclaim. Memoirs by Jennifer Finney Boylan, Janet Mock and others are widely read. Numerous documentaries and shows on public, cable and commercial TV have presented the lives of transgender people in a sympathetic light. Barack Obama was the first US president to express support for transgender civil rights. The US military is allowing transgender people to serve openly. The US Department of Veterans Affairs has an initiative in place to provide appropriate services to LGBT veterans. In my state of Connecticut, we have seen the passage of a transgender civil rights law, the development of school guidelines for fair treatment of transgender students, and a decision by the insurance commissioner that health insurance plans originating in the state must include coverage for transgender health care.

Teens and young adults have access to a large array of information on the internet. They can watch videos that others have produced charting their personal journeys of gender transition. There are support groups in some communities and many online chat opportunities. As a result, I find that young people who realize they are transgender expect to access hormone treatment or surgery very quickly. This creates pressure on parents and helping professionals to learn a lot in a short time, to come to terms with their fears, and to make decisions that they know will have a long-term impact without the luxury of long-term contemplation.

There have also been shifts in recent years in the response of the professional community to transgender youth. Mental health professionals working extensively with gender variant children and teens are recognizing gender certainty at younger ages. They are advocating for children to be free to live in the gender they feel they are. Johanna Olson-Kennedy (2016) and her colleagues in California initiate cross-sex hormone therapy for some teens at ages younger than 16. The reduction in the number of Americans without health insurance, along with increased coverage of transgender health services, has begun to improve access to treatment in the United States. Previously, whether a family could obtain the treatment their transgender child needed was entirely dependent on what they could afford, unfairly excluding those of lesser economic means. Connecticut is not alone among states that require insurance plans to include transgender health care.[1] The exclusion of transgender health coverage is discrimination against a stigmatized and misunderstood minority. Efforts to educate citizens and government officials about transgender lives are important steps toward creating access to services.

School and workplace realities have also changed significantly. Some states have passed transgender civil rights laws, which require schools and employers to treat their transgender students and employees fairly. Many businesses have adopted transgender non-discrimination policies without waiting for a government mandate, as they realize they are most successful if they create a work environment that is welcoming to all. Schools often address this issue *after* they have had their first transgender student. Most are well intentioned; they learn as they go and are then more welcoming for future students. Numerous organizations are working to increase awareness and fairness for trans[2] people, in schools, workplaces and other contexts.

When I first began working with the parents of transgender teens, even the most supportive parents wanted to keep their child's gender exploration a private matter, only discussed in therapy or at home, and not shared publicly until they had all had a long time to think things over. Compare that with what we hear from a family that was interviewed for National Public Radio in 2015, talking

---

1 The National Center for Transgender Equality keeps up-to-date information on health insurance and other transgender civil rights matters: http://transequality. org/know-your-rights

2 'Trans' is often used as an acceptable and respectful shorter version of 'transgender,' especially in speaking. Sometimes you will see it written with an asterisk: trans*. The asterisk is not intended to indicate a footnote, but to indicate that 'trans' is a term encompassing many different people and experiences.

about their 4-year-old, Jackie, whose birth name was Jack. Here's Mary, her mom, talking about what happened on May 15, 2014:

> 'Jackie just looked really, really sad; sadder than a 3½-year-old should look,' Mary says. 'This weight that looked like it weighed more than she did, something she had to say and I didn't know what that was. So I asked. I said, "Jackie, are you sad that you're not going to school today?" And Jackie was really quiet and put her head down and said, "No, I'm sad because I'm a boy."'
>
> Mary was taken aback. Her youngest had been wearing her big sister's dresses regularly and enjoyed donning pink boots. But this was new.
>
> She wanted to confirm. 'You're really not happy being a boy?' she asked.
>
> 'I thought a little bit longer and I said, "Well, are you happy being you?" And that made Jackie smile,' she says. 'And I felt like for that moment, that was all that really mattered. That was "The Day."'
>
> Mary took her to a chain drugstore, and Jackie asked for elastic hair bands. Her hair wasn't long enough yet, but Mary put Jackie's hair up in five makeshift ponytails.
>
> 'And I've never seen such a happy child,' she remembers. 'To go from maybe an hour before this, this child who looks so sad, to that, I felt like I'd done something right by her.' (Westervelt 2015)

In the months that followed, they started talking over girl names, with help from Jackie's pre-K teacher. On her fourth birthday, the family sang happy birthday for the first time to Jackie.

Notice their acceptance that such a young child knows who she is and needs to live authentically, full time. These parents are not naïve about the difficulties they and their child face. The story goes on:

> It's only been a little more than a year since Jack became Jackie. Neither of her parents has any illusions about the potential

> struggles ahead. Transgender people have alarmingly high
> rates of depression, substance abuse and suicide. 'There will be
> more challenges, certainly, as Jackie gets older and gets around
> more kids,' James [Jackie's dad] says. 'Then puberty, and dating,
> and the challenges will be like a very steep curve. But I'm hoping
> that by the time she gets there, I hope, one, we've given her
> the tools and two, that there's more acceptance of this issue.'
> (Westervelt 2015)

James and Mary encountered this challenge at a time when there
were many supports in their community for children who are gender
variant and for their families. They are comfortable letting others
know who their child is, including a national radio audience. They
do not seem to have an internalized sense of stigma about their
child's gender identity, but they remain aware that others may be
prejudiced and unkind.

As a gay man who came out in the 1970s, I brought a lot of
valuable personal experience to my work with transgender clients.
While gender identity and sexual orientation are two different
aspects of who a person is, and the challenges faced by gay and
transgender people differ, there are some similarities. From my life
experience, I understood what it is like to know something about
yourself as a teenager that is stigmatized, and to somehow at the
same time keep this information out of your self-awareness. I knew
what it is like to be teased, in my case not too often, for being gender
nonconforming. Adults were not especially safe in this regard. My
eighth grade gym teacher called me 'Alice' as an insult when I was
clumsy at baseball. I spent much of my time in gym class avoiding
being noticed. I knew what it is like to not fit in with others of your
gender, not share in the excitement they might be feeling about
dating and sex, and feel vaguely ashamed about that.

When I did come out during my college years, it was at a time
when homosexuality was considered sick or sinful by many, gay sex
was illegal, and few expected gay men and lesbians to find true love,
raise healthy children or have a successful career. Gay marriage was
a pipe dream, although not one I particularly concerned myself with.

To some extent I relished being outside the norm, outside the law, and part of a movement to help the rest of society loosen up their rigid ideas about identity, sexuality and relationships. I believed that I could be happy in love and manage to have a decent life, but not necessarily that I would have the family support, professional success, long-term relationship and joy of having children that I have in fact experienced. I am fortunate to have had an exciting time coming out and a relatively easy ride since.

In my years as a therapist for gay and lesbian clients, I was able to see firsthand how things turned out for those who continued to hide their sexuality well into adulthood, and the forces that conspired to press them to do so. I saw how important it was for people to have a safe place to talk about their need to be authentic, their fear of how others would respond, and to figure out how to proceed safely. Despite the risks of family rejection or job loss, most of my closeted gay and lesbian clients chose to come out. And despite whatever losses ensued, which were in some cases significant but most often less severe than expected, there were no regrets. They came to the conclusion that it was best to find out where the actual rejections would be, then cut their losses and move on. I found out that negative family responses tend to soften over time. Legal protections were advancing in tandem with greater societal acceptance, and each person's coming out added to the momentum of increased acceptance and respect. I came to appreciate how fortunate I was when I came out that I was otherwise a person of privilege: a white, able-bodied and healthy male student at an elite college in a politically liberal urban area, with a stable family background, no debt, and parents who loved and supported me even though they struggled with fears about my future as a gay man. I always kept in mind that many of my clients faced multiple challenges, so their coming out process had to be more cautious than mine and was not necessarily going to be fun. By the time I was working as a therapist, AIDS was an additional threat that many of us faced, and for some a complicating factor in the coming out process.

My first experience of getting to know a transgender person well was in my work as a 'buddy' in the early years of AIDS Project New Haven (APNH). As a gay man aware of and fearful of AIDS, volunteering with APNH was a way to learn more about the disease and how to protect myself, while at the same time providing help to those who were already infected. At that time there were no medications to halt the advance of HIV, so people with AIDS did not expect to survive long. Mariela was a feisty and vivacious Latina who had lived life on the edge. She was charming and funny and told amazing stories about her dangerous escapades. The more time I spent with her, the more I understood that she was simply a woman rather than a man who had become a woman. Her physiology was irrelevant to who she truly was. Her family, though from a conservative religious culture, fully accepted her as female and did not stigmatize her for the unconventional life she had led. They welcomed me as well in my role as a support for Mariela.

Mariela had a dinner party for me on my birthday at her apartment. A few months later I was at her hospital bedside when she passed away. She was someone who had been brave and self-assured, with a good dose of humor, in the face of extreme prejudice and hardship. She showed me that a person can live happily and lovingly in the midst of a catastrophe. When I see young trans people and their parents able to celebrate who they are, rather than merely tolerate or accept their difference, I am reminded of Mariela. She was part of a generation of courageous trans people who paved the way for the benefits many transgender youth are able to access today.

My work with transgender teens and young adults took off after I started seeing my first few trans teen clients in 2004. I already had a website in place so that LGBT adults seeking a therapist within the queer[3] community could find me. Soon I was getting contacted

---

3   'Queer' is a historically derogatory term that has been appropriated by the
    community for use in a prideful way. It is now an affirming umbrella term
    encompassing all with unconventional gender identity and/or sexuality.

directly by teens themselves, or by parents who said, 'My child found you online and wants to come see you.' Some of my referrals came from the Connecticut Department of Children and Families. Sadly, many LGBT youth are rejected by their families for gender nonconforming behavior.

After working with numerous families with transgender youth, I realized there was a core of information that parents and guardians needed, regardless of their ethnic, educational, economic and racial backgrounds. In 2011 I published *Helping Your Transgender Teen: A Guide for Parents* to help parents who were just learning that their teen is or may be transgender. The book covers: basic information parents need about gender identity; ways to nurture your child and address your fears and concerns; and information on the transition steps that may be taken by teens who identify as transgender. Since 2011, thousands of copies of the book have been purchased, and hundreds more distributed to organizations and individuals that work with youth. I have received many emails from parents who found the book helpful at a time of crisis. It is short, direct and easy to read.

In recent years the volume of inquiries and referrals has mushroomed. I receive emails from parents, teens and young adults all over the United States and occasionally from other countries. I try to offer encouragement and find local resources for them whenever possible. For some families in areas where trans-specific support is not yet available, traveling to a trans youth and family conference is the best option. I provide links to conferences and national and global support organizations on my website,[4] along with links to sites that help locate experienced therapists. Many of these conferences, organizations and links are listed in Appendix B. To help address the need for knowledgeable providers, I have been offering training for mental health clinicians. A number of schools have invited me to train their staff to work supportively with transgender students.

---

4   www.CounselingTransgenderYouth.com

With this new book I am aiming to reach mental health providers who have transgender teen and young adult clients, as well as those who are training to become mental health clinicians. Much of the information in this book will be useful to parents, educators, medical professionals and others who want to learn how to help transgender teens and young adults.

The second chapter in this section of the book focuses on the themes of authenticity and safety, which loom large in the process of helping transgender youth. The following section (**Foundations**) has three chapters providing basic information about transgender identities. At the end of each of these and subsequent chapters you will find suggested reading lists and videos for further exploration. I especially recommend the memoirs, videos and blogs created by trans people themselves. The third section (**Assessment**) details the components of evaluating transgender youth and addressing any mental health concerns. The fourth section of the book (**Transition**) discusses gender transition and referral for medical interventions. The final section (**Youth in Context**) is a guide to family therapy, advocacy at school, and helping trans youth face additional challenges. In the **Appendices** are resources for learning more and getting assistance, as well as examples of medical referral letters your clients may need from you.

Whatever your reason for picking up this book, I hope you find it helpful! Please let me know. My contact information is at the start of Appendix B.

CHAPTER 2

Authenticity and Safety

The first step to prepare yourself to help transgender youth is to examine your own experiences with the struggle between authenticity and safety. This will enable you to bring more emotional depth to your understanding of transgender teens and young adults and their families.

Authenticity and safety are prominent themes in the lives of LGBT teens and adults. We feel the urge to be our true selves and yet we are aware that danger lurks when we come out. We are at risk of being hurt emotionally or physically. We are at risk of losing family connections, social connections, jobs or fair treatment by others. The more we fear these losses, the less likely we are to come out. At the same time, we know that coming out helps all of us in the long term. This conflict has been present since the early days of the gay liberation movement. For example, in the Foreword of the 20th anniversary edition of *Out of the Closets*, originally published in 1972, John D'Emilio writes:

> I would argue that the revolutionary aspirations of these young lesbian and gay radicals are directly responsible for their signal achievement: their willingness to burst out of the closet and to come out in a public, uncompromising way. For all the change

that had occurred before Stonewall,[1] the prohibitions against homosexuality were still so deeply embedded in Western culture and the punishments attached to exposure remained so great that few gay men and lesbians were willing to affiliate with the homophile movement... But, because this cohort of gays and lesbians was committed to revolution, because they had broken with the values of American society and scorned the rewards that success in America offered, they were virtually immune to the penalties that kept homosexuals in line. (D'Emilio 1992, p.xx)

The editors of that book, Karla Jay and Allen Young, in their introduction to the new edition, emphasize the value the movement continues to place on authenticity over safety. Authentic expression initially creates increased risk but eventually leads to greater safety for all: 'Thus, it is as true today as it was two decades ago that all lesbians and gay men must come out of the closet if any of us is to be free' (Jay and Young 1992, p.xxxiii). Robin Ochs speaks similarly about coming out for bisexuals: 'We must weigh the costs and benefits of coming out... We come out because the alternative to disclosure is misunderstanding' (Ochs and Rowley 2005, p.16).

My adult lesbian and gay clients have uniformly felt that their coming out was worthwhile, even those who lost important family connections in the process. They felt it was better to be who you are and know where you stand than to be living a lie to maintain family support. What was their support worth if the person they were supporting was not really you? I am reminded of Eleanor Roosevelt's words: 'Courage is more exhilarating than fear and in the long run it is easier' (Roosevelt 1960, p.41).

Contemporary transgender writers, based on their experiences with this challenge, have continued to promote authenticity. Jamison Green talks about the terror trans men felt in the 1990s about the dangers of coming out. For him 'the potential benefit to

---

1   The Stonewall Riots, which took place in New York in 1969, are often viewed as the start of the gay liberation movement in the United States.

gender-variant people outweighed the risk' (Green 2004, p.179). In *Redefining Realness*, Janet Mock writes: 'I can't help but marvel at the resiliency of trans people who sacrificed so much to be seen and accepted as they are' (2014, p.235). And in Matt Kailey's words:

> If we don't speak up, if we don't make ourselves visible and let our voices be heard, if we don't come out and let people know who we are, our lives, and our destinies, will continue to be decided for us. We'll continue to be discriminated against, receive substandard medical care, lose our jobs, our housing—even our lives. (Kailey 2005, p.116)

As I will discuss in Chapter 11, the apparent conflict between authenticity and safety is the central dilemma for many families of transgender youth. Take a moment now to reflect on your own experience with authenticity and safety.

SELF-REFLECTION

Think of a time in your life when there was something you knew to be true about yourself that you were afraid to disclose to others. It may have been an aspect of who you were. It may have been a particular interest you had that others would have disdained. Perhaps there was someone you wanted as a friend who was not well regarded by your peers. Perhaps there was an aspect of self-expression you stifled to avoid disapproval. An authenticity challenge can be about something major, like sexuality or gender identity. Or it may be about something seemingly minor that you fear would affect how others regard you.

Once you have thought of a time when you faced an authenticity challenge, take a few moments to remember everything you can about that time. How old were you? What were your life circumstances? Whose opinions mattered most to you? Were there aspects of yourself you felt confident about? Were there ways in which you deeply doubted your worth?

Now focus on the specific aspect of your authentic self that you were afraid to disclose. Whose response did you fear the most? What did you imagine to be the possible negative consequences of being your true self? What would you have hoped for as a positive outcome if you 'came out' about it? Would you have been satisfied just to be free to be yourself, or did you need to have a supportive response from others? What were you at risk of losing if you let others know this truth about you?

Reflect on how you handled your dilemma at that time. Think about the stress you experienced in making that decision. You may have chosen to keep this part of yourself secret, or to stifle it altogether, or you may have come out with it. Remember what you chose to do and what the outcome was. If you did disclose, how did the response compare to what you had expected? Were there particular responses from certain individuals or groups that had the most impact on you? If you got negative responses, were you glad anyway that you had chosen to be your authentic self, or did you wish you had kept things quiet? If you did not reveal this aspect of yourself at that time, how did you feel about your decision afterward? How do you feel about it now?

The purpose of this exercise is to get you to think about how it may feel for your transgender clients when steps toward being more authentic bring a risk of danger, and decisions to stay safe require stifling part or all of their authentic self. Things that seem clear and self-evident in the safety of a therapy office may be terrifying in daily life. A decision to disclose personal information is irreversible: you can't take it back and you can't be sure that your information is going to be kept private. For teenagers and young adults who are still figuring out the social landscape, these challenges may be enormous; the resultant stress often leads to anxiety, depression or behavior problems. For parents, who want to nurture their child and protect them as well, this dilemma may seem unsolvable.

AUTHENTICITY AND SAFETY IN ADOLESCENCE

Adolescence is a time of identity integration (Erikson 1968). It is a time to ask, 'Who am I? Where do I fit in? How am I similar to or different from my family and my peers?' Many use their teen years to try out different presentations and affiliations. For teens who realize that their gender identity and their body don't match, being authentically themselves becomes of paramount importance. But trying out being their real selves is not a simple matter. For transgender youth, 'there is the additional challenge of integrating a complex gender identity with their cultural and ethnic backgrounds, personal characteristics, and family circumstances' (Grossman and D'Augelli 2006, p.113). Their distress about the discordance between who they feel they are inside and who they appear to be on the outside increases. They are painfully aware that their parents and peers may have great difficulty accepting them. They struggle with disclosure, perhaps hinting about it at first, or trying out an identity of lesbian or gay, to see what fits and how much others will understand and accept.

Identifying as transgender, or even questioning one's gender identity, is an experience that most young people do not have in common with their parents or guardians. They are likely to have few, if any, peers in their community who feel like them. Transgender portrayals in mainstream media are increasing. Many are positive, some are sensationalized and most stick to one narrative: I knew when I was three years old; my parents could see I was not a typical boy or girl; my parents and I have been struggling to come to terms with this ever since, at great emotional cost (see, for example, the ABC News 2012 *20/20* documentary 'Boys Will Be Girls'). The presence of this narrative in mainstream media is welcome, but limited, in that it does not provide any role models or sense of belonging for trans youth whose experiences differ from this new norm.

In the absence of family, peer and societal support, transgender individuals are likely to first conclude that there is something wrong with them and with the few others they may be aware of who are like them. In addition, transgender and gender nonconforming (TGNC) individuals may experience *nonaffirmation*:

> Nonaffirmation occurs when one's internal sense of gender identity is not affirmed by others. For instance, a trans woman may be addressed as 'sir' when making a purchase or answering the phone, or might be referred to with her former male name by an individual not yet fully comfortable with her gender identity. TGNC individuals who do not identify as either male or female (e.g., individuals who identify as genderqueer) may also experience a sense of nonaffirmation as people in their life are unable to refer to them in gender neutral ways. (Testa *et al.* 2015, p.66)

Awareness of hostility toward trans people leads to expectations of greater hostility and rejection should one be more self-affirming in public. For many, the result is deep internalization of negative attitudes about their gender identity. Others are more resilient. They are able to take pride in their identity, stand up to oppression, navigate difficult relationships, access resources, collaborate with others in the transgender and ally communities, and maintain a hopeful outlook (Hendricks and Testa 2012).

Some youth are fortunate to live in communities and families that are relatively open-minded about gender presentation. Young people sense this and are able to assess reasonably well whether it is safe for them to try out authentic nonconforming gender expression at home or at school. Those who feel safe enough to do so are able to use the experience to better understand who they are and whether they want to proceed with gender transition. Those who lack a safe outlet for gender expression are likely to experience greater distress. Many are able to get some of the support and information they need online. My years of working with teens and young adults has taught me that online friendships can be as nurturing and important in a young person's life as the friendships they have in their local community.

For transgender youth who don't feel safe in their community, online friendships may be their sole or certainly their most important source of support. For some youth who do not feel safe in high school, going away to college is an opportunity to experience a welcoming, inclusive environment. But not all youth have the means to go away to college or to relocate safely and successfully. And many younger teens do not feel they can wait that long even if college is likely in their future. In Chapter 12 I will discuss the ways that middle and high schools can create safety for transgender students, even those who do not feel safe to be themselves at home. For now, it is important to keep in mind that grappling with gender identity in an unsafe environment can take a great toll.

FOUNDATIONS

CHAPTER 3

Four Dimensions of Transgender Identity

There are four facets of identity and sexuality to keep in mind as you learn about transgender identities. These are:

- assigned sex
- gender identity
- gender expression
- sexual orientation.

ASSIGNED SEX

A newborn's sex is determined at birth, based on the appearance of external genitalia. *Assigned sex* is a binary construct—there are only two choices offered. This term is preferred over 'biological sex', which implies that this determination is an absolute statement about the infant's biology. The terms *birth sex* or *natal sex* can be stand-ins for 'assigned sex.'

If we reduce sex biologically to only male and female, there are many individuals who are left out. These include intersex children who may have ambiguous external genitalia or internal and external genitalia of different sexes. There are also children with chromosomal arrangements other than XX or XY, or with genetic differences that lead to mixed-sex biology. For these children a determination of female or male does not reflect the complexity of their sex (Fausto-Sterling 2000). Sometimes these genetic differences are referred to as 'disorders of sex development' (National Health Service 2014).

Even children who are known at birth to be of uncertain sex are assigned to one sex or the other within the binary system. Our culture does not have room at this time for a child to be understood as neither male nor female in their early years. In the best circumstances, intersex children are given free rein to express their gender as they grow up (Diamond and Beh 2008). Over time these children will be able to affirm the gender identity that feels right to them and to seek whatever medical interventions they may wish to have. The recent and past practice of performing surgery on the genitals of intersex children to make them conform to typical male or female appearance has been strongly opposed by adults who are intersex and the community that supports them. Organization Intersex International, InterACT and Intersex Society of North America all take the position that medical interventions can wait until the child is old enough to participate in the discussion.

GENDER IDENTITY

Gender identity is our inner sense of whether we are female, male, neither or both. Awareness of gender begins when we are quite young:

> Most 2-year-olds already know whether they are boys or girls and can identify strangers as 'mommies' or 'daddies.' By the age of 3, children know that daddy has a penis and that mommy has breasts, and they consistently apply gender labels. They know that blocks, hammers, trucks, and wrestling are for boys, while pots and pans, dolls, and aprons are for girls, and they generally avoid playing with toys associated with the other gender. (Menvielle, Tuerk and Perrin 2005, p.38)

Usually a child's gender identity matches their assigned sex and the child does not give the concept much thought. But those who are transgender may express as early as age three or four that they are of the other gender, that they feel they should have other sexual organs than the ones they have, or that they expect to grow up into an adult of the opposite sex (Cohen-Kettenis and Pfäfflin 2003; Olson-Kennedy *et al.* 2016; Pleak 2009). Diane Ehrensaft (2016) gives an example of a 4-year-old wanting opposite-sex genitals. Genny Beemyn and Susan Rankin (2011), in their phone interviews with 75 transgender adults, found the mean age for first realizing they were different from others of their assigned sex was 5.4 years old.

Until recently, most parents simply assured their children that their gender was the same as their assigned sex, they could be happy and fulfilled in their assigned sex, and they need not feel constrained by it. As you read in Chapter 1, some parents now respond much more open-mindedly to children who express an identity different than the one they were assigned at birth. My belief is that all children should be made aware that there are some people whose gender identity does not match their assigned sex, and that those people have options for self-expression and, if necessary, physical changes as they get older. Transgender young people who are aware of this can then feel hopeful about living an authentic life. I have listed a few children's books at the end of this chapter that help convey these ideas to young children. There are more books like these published each year.

Gender identity exists along a spectrum. At either end of the spectrum are those who feel firmly that they are female or they are male and are comfortable being viewed that way by others. But there are many people whose sense of themselves is neither female nor male: perhaps a blend of the two, or a third gender, or no gender at all. These identities are referred to as non-binary identities. Some of the terms individuals have used to describe their non-binary identities are:

- genderqueer, genderfluid
- agender, bigender
- gender neutral

- transmasculine, transfeminine
- third gender
- pangender, polygender.

See Appendix A for provisional definitions of these terms. Keep in mind that these terms are constantly invented and evolving. It is safe to say you cannot assume you know what a particular individual means when they use one of these terms, other than that they are in the non-binary realm of gender identity. If you know the person well enough to do so, it is best to respectfully inquire how they arrived at using that particular term.

People who have a gender identity that is different from the one they were assigned at birth often choose a name that is different from the one they were given at birth and ask to be addressed by pronouns that are different from the ones people have been using for them. Those who identify in the gender opposite the one they were assigned at birth will most often request pronouns of the opposite gender while those with a non-binary gender identity have a number of choices. The most common set of pronouns used by people with non-binary gender identity at the time of this writing is they/them/their. It can take some practice to use these pronouns comfortably to refer to one person, but after a while it becomes easy to do so. We already do this routinely when referring to someone who is not present and whose gender is unknown or unimportant to the point we are making. For example I may say, 'I met with the director this morning and they told me they have no additional suggestions.' If you heard me say that, you would most likely not find it awkward or correct me by suggesting I should have specified the person's gender and used the singular verb 'has.' While we are used to referring to someone this way when the person is not present and is not known to us, it is more of a challenge to use 'they' pronouns when the person is present or they are someone well known to us. In this book I will be using the pronouns 'they, them and their' freely in the singular. Perhaps this will help you get accustomed to the sound and use of these pronouns in referring to one person. I have found that the reflexive pronoun most commonly used in this set is 'themself,' but this may change.

Some non-binary individuals use pronouns that were created specifically to refer to people with non-binary gender identities. The most common of these pronoun sets is ze/hir/hirs/hirself, pronounced 'zee,' 'heer,' and so on. There are other sets beginning with 'xe' and 'ey,' and perhaps more to be invented. So far, none of these sets of invented pronouns has found widespread use. It is as important to do your best to respect and use a non-binary person's pronouns, as it is for the person who has transitioned to a new gender and wants you to use 'he' instead of 'she' or vice versa. Your effort to do so matters more than success at doing so 100 percent of the time. Your willingness to correct yourself when you hear your error or if it is pointed out to you will also be appreciated.

GENDER EXPRESSION

There are many ways we communicate our gender to others. *Gender expression* is a person's presentation of self to others as masculine, feminine, neither or both. Many of the 'rules' about what constitutes expression of which gender are culturally based. Some of the ways we express our gender seem to come naturally to us and some are learned. Those of us who feel in sync with our assigned sex often look to older peers and adults of the same gender as role models. Those whose natural way of being or whose interests do not match what their family or society expects of them in terms of gender are often told or shown by others that their natural way of being is shameful. To gain approval they may strive to fit in with the gender expectations of their culture. Some succeed at this fully or partially and others do not. Those who do not conform often experience ongoing criticism, rejection, bullying or violence as they grow up and even in adulthood. In a 2012 review of research on pressure to conform to gender stereotypes, Gray, Carter and Levitt found that boys' gender expression is policed more tightly than that of girls. Arnold Grossman and Anthony D'Augelli (2006) report that gender-atypical boys are most often the targets of verbal and physical abuse.

Many of these gender expectations vary from culture to culture or within a given culture in different time periods (Teich 2012). Examples include:

- the way we dress
- the way we cut and style our hair
- whether and how we wear makeup or jewelry
- the way we walk and move and sit
- the way we speak and gesture with our hands
- games, hobbies and work we engage in or prefer.

While cultures worldwide have clearly established norms for female and male gender expression, and some have an established third gender with its own idiosyncracies, there is wide variation in acceptance for those who stray from gender norms (Teich 2012). There are no cultures other than some parts of the queer community that have recognizable indicators for non-binary identities. As a result it is impossible for non-binary individuals to signal to those outside of queer culture that they want to be understood as non-binary without having to announce and explain their identity.

Transgender individuals are those for whom these three aspects of identity do not line up. In other words, their gender identity or gender expression diverges from their assigned sex. Julia Serano (2007, p.80) describes her awareness of being female this way: 'It seems as if, on some level, my brain expects my body to be female.' She prefers the term 'subconscious sex' rather than 'gender identity,' as the latter may suggest to some that the affirmed gender is a chosen identity rather than a visceral sense. *Transsexual* is a term that describes people whose gender identity is the opposite of their assigned sex, within the binary system. This term is used less often by younger transgender people. Some may find it too clinical, much as gay people let go of the term 'homosexual' many years ago. Other ways of describing people whose gender identity is the binary opposite of their assigned sex is *male to female (MTF)*, or *female to male (FTM)*. Another respectful term is *trans woman* or *trans man*, using the term that references the individual's affirmed gender identity. In all cases, it is best to find out how an individual identifies themself and to use that language when speaking about them. If you are uncertain, you can always rely on gender-neutral language, such as using the word 'person' and using 'they' pronouns, or simply referring to the person by name.

Cisgender individuals are those for whom these three aspects of identity do line up. In other words, their gender identity and gender expression are in accordance with their assigned sex. Most people are cisgender and most cisgender people take their gender identity for granted, since it is in accordance with what others expect.

As with gender identity, gender expression exists on a spectrum from feminine to masculine. Most people have interests, personal styles and behaviors that range across the spectrum of feminine and masculine gender expression. Some cultures are more accepting of this variation than others. As we continue to see a loosening up of expectations and limitations based on gender, it is likely that variations in gender expression will no longer be as significant a factor in understanding transgender identity. At this time in Western culture, the last holdout seems to be the view that men who wear feminine clothing are 'crossdressing,' while women who wear masculine clothing are not. *Crossdresser* is an identity that currently falls under the transgender umbrella, and almost always refers to someone assigned male. For a cogent dissection of why men who wear what are considered women's clothing, or who embrace other signifiers of femininity, elicit such troubled and troubling responses, see 'Crossdressing: Demystifying Femininity and Rethinking "Male" Privilege' in *Whipping Girl* (Serano 2007).

SEXUAL ORIENTATION

While gender identity refers to who you are inside, *sexual orientation* refers to who you find attractive. The most common words to describe sexual orientations are based on the idea that a person has a clear gender identity of female or male, and their sexual, emotional and romantic attractions are to males, females or both in varying degrees. These terms are located within the realm of binary gender identities. Thus we understand *heterosexual* to refer to opposite-gender attractions, *lesbian, gay* and *homosexual* to refer to same-gender attractions, and *bisexual* to refer to attractions to females and males. It is generally assumed, but not always the case, that the objects of a person's attractions are the same whether we are talking about sexual, emotional or romantic attractions, and that a person's sexual behaviors are fully in accordance with their attractions. Understanding someone's sexual orientation requires inclusion of all aspects of these attractions and behaviors.

Many people are comfortable using one of the words highlighted above to describe their sexual orientation. Some prefer to have no label at all. And many, especially many young people, find other terms to describe their orientation, such as pansexual, asexual and heteroflexible, or they use combinations such as asexual biromantic. *Pansexual* individuals are those whose sexual attractions are not based on the gender of the person they find attractive. Instead, the pansexual person is attracted to other personal qualities or aspects of an individual's appearance. *Asexual* people experience little or no sexual attraction. But if they, for example, feel emotionally or romantically attracted to both females and males, they may describe themselves as *asexual biromantic. Heteroflexible* is a term used to describe those who are primarily heterosexual but occasionally are attracted to, or engage in sex with, same-gender partners. A *heteroflexible panromantic* is someone whose sexual attractions and behaviors are largely heterosexual, but who experiences romantic yearnings for others regardless of gender. As with the many words used and invented to describe non-binary gender identities, it is not safe to assume you know what these terms mean for the person who uses them. If you want to understand, you will need to ask.

Just as cisgender people can be straight, gay, lesbian or bisexual, so too can transgender people (Beemyn and Rankin 2011; Teich 2012). There is 'little to no consistent data regarding the sexual orientation of this population; indeed, data collected by the transgender community is beginning to demonstrate that transgender individuals are as sexually diverse as any other demographic' (Meier and Labuski 2013, p.309). Many people assume that those who transition in gender are always heterosexual in their affirmed gender, attracted to the now 'opposite' sex. They are surprised to learn that many trans women, for example, are primarily or exclusively attracted to women and may identify as lesbian; and many trans men are primarily or exclusively attracted to men and may identify as gay. We do not have established terms for the sexual orientation of those whose gender identity is non-binary. So far there is not a commonly used term to indicate a person of non-binary identity who is exclusively or primarily attracted to males, or to females. Keep in mind that many individuals are not interested in labeling their sexual orientation. And some trans people experience a shift in their sexual orientation during transition (Davis and Meier 2013). Hill-Meyer and Scarborough explain:

> Some of us find that after we transition we are attracted to people of a gender we were not interested in before... Shifting preferences could be related to hormones, but it could also be about the way we see ourselves and what kinds of relationships we feel socially comfortable in. (Hill-Meyer and Scarborough 2014, pp.364–5)

While the most commonly used sexual orientation descriptors (such as gay and straight) do not work for those whose gender identity is non-binary or uncertain, pansexual and other non-binary sexual orientation terms can easily fit those with non-binary gender identity. Again, keep in mind that many people don't want or need a label for their sexual orientation. As a clinician working with transgender youth, the important point is that sexual orientation is a complex aspect of identity which is independent of gender identity.

PREVALENCE OF TRANSGENDER YOUTH

The percentage of the population who identify as transgender cannot be estimated accurately at this time. Colt Keo-Meier and Christine Labuski summarize the challenges this way:

The difficulties, as we see them, stem from two main sources: (1) though a general 'trans' sensibility exists in both the United States and worldwide, there are currently few measurable and/or standardized criteria (e.g. physical, social, political, etc.) regarding what might or *should* constitute a transgender person; and (2) problems with locating and accounting for this population are compounded by the relative invisibility through which many transgender individuals exist in their daily lives. (Meier and Labuski 2013, p.289)

They cite estimates ranging from 1 in 100,000 to 1 in 500 to as high as 2–3 percent of the population, noting that the population estimates they reviewed generally reported a prevalence of less than 1 percent. The authors go on to suggest a number of reasons that these figures may reflect under-reporting:

- Sample sizes are small.
- Most of the studies only count individuals treated at gender clinics, missing many:
  › Some transgender individuals avoid clinics.
  › Some transgender individuals do not have access to medical treatment, especially trans people of color and those of limited financial means.
- Some transgender people do not disclose their transgender identity to others, preferring to be known only in their affirmed gender. They may simply identify as female or male and not as transgender.

In contrast, 'when trans researchers start measuring members of their own population, larger sample sizes are typically collected' (Meier and Labuski 2013, p.301). The 2–3 percent figure mentioned above is from one such study by the National Transgender Advocacy Coalition in the United States.

In my own work, as well as in my supervision of other clinicians, numerous instances of a group of transgender teens in a single high school have come to my attention. The numbers that I have encountered suggest an incidence between 0.3 percent and 1.00 percent. This does not include the students in these schools who have not yet come out publicly as transgender, or those who are seriously questioning their gender identity. Similarly, a survey of adults in Massachusetts reported that 0.5 percent of the respondents identified themselves as transgender (Conron *et al.* 2012). I expect the number of out transgender youth will continue to grow as there is greater awareness and acceptance of transgender identity, and the reported prevalence of transgender youth will increase. As for differences in birth-assigned gender of transgender youth seeking services, a review of 97 youth at Boston Children's Hospital's gender clinic reported a close to 1:1 ratio between those assigned male:female (Spack *et al.* 2012).

FOR FURTHER EXPLORATION

Children's books

I am Jazz, by Jazz Jennings and Jessica Herthel, Dial Books for Young Readers, 2014.

Jacob's New Dress, by Sarah and Ian Hoffman, Albert Whitman and Company, 2014.

Michael and Me, by Margaret Baker-Street, Xlibris, 2014.

Stacey's Not A Girl, by Colt Keo-Meier and Jesse Yang, 2016.

Who Are You? The Kid's Guide to Gender Identity, by Brook Pessin-Whedbee and Naomi Bardoff, Jessica Kingsley Publishers, 2016.

Other books

Sexing the Body: Gender Politics and the Construction of Sexuality, by Anne Fausto-Sterling, Basic Books, 2012.

The Sexual Spectrum: Why We're All Different, by Olive Skene Johnson, Raincoast Books, 2004.

Trans Bodies, Trans Selves: A Resource for the Transgender Community, edited by Laura Erickson-Schroth, Oxford University Press, 2014.

Transgender 101: A Simple Guide to a Complex Issue, by Nicholas Teich, Columbia University Press, 2012.

Transgender Explained for Those Who Are Not, by Joanne Herman, Author House, 2009.

Blogs and video

Alok Vaid-Menon is a non-binary transfeminine writer, performance artist, and community organizer. Their blog is available at https://returnthegayze.com, with links to essays and videos.

Jacob Tobia's writing and videos about non-binary identity are available at www.jacobtobia.com

'Neutrois Nonsense' is a blog about non-binary gender identities. Available at www.neutrois.me

Sophie Labelle's comics and children's books can be found at www.assignedmale.com

'The T Word' is a documentary about the lives of seven transgender youth. Available at www.mtv.com/full-episodes/e1b1ow/the-t-word-laverne-cox-presents-the-t-word-season-1-ep-special

CHAPTER 4

The Impact of Stigma on Transgender and Non-Binary Youth

One of my earliest jobs was as a mental health worker in a community mental health center serving economically disadvantaged people. Our day treatment program provided group and family therapy for individuals with disabling mental health problems. This experience, coupled with personal reflection on challenges I have faced as a gay man, taught me to look at the larger context when providing mental health care for people from stigmatized groups. My education in clinical social work, with its biopsychosocial perspective, gave added emphasis to the impact of political and societal oppression. Similarly, the American Psychological Association has noted:

> The concerns of transgender and gender-variant persons are inextricably tied to issues of social justice, which have historically been important to APA. The stigmatization and discrimination experienced by transgender people affect virtually all aspects of their lives, including physical safety, psychological well-being, access to services, and basic human rights. (Schneider *et al.* 2009, p.2)

This chapter looks at the impact of stigma on a transgender individual's safety, and the types of responses they are likely to face when they choose to live authentically. In particular, I will discuss:

- discrimination against transgender people
- intersectionality
- homelessness
- microaggression.

The chapter concludes with specific suggestions for therapists to communicate respect, inclusion and affirmation of their transgender clients.

DISCRIMINATION

The 2015 US Transgender Survey (USTS) was released in 2016 by the National Center for Transgender Equality. Over 27,000 transgender and gender nonconforming people from all 50 states, the District of Columbia and Puerto Rico, as well as US territories and military bases participated in the survey. By comparison, Meier and Labuski (2013) point out that most studies by cisgender researchers have had sample sizes of 100 or less. The USTS quantifies the discrimination and violence transgender people face in the United States.

Respondents experienced high rates of harassment at school, on the job, and in places of public accommodation such as hotels, restaurants, buses, airports and government agencies. They faced discrimination when they sought employment or health care and when they interacted with the police. The highest rates of discrimination were reported by transgender people of color. Roughly a third of the survey's participants have experienced homelessness at some point. A quarter of those who were homeless avoided shelters because they feared mistreatment.The summary of the Transgender Survey reports:

A staggering 39% of respondents experienced serious psychological distress in the month prior to completing the survey, compared with only 5% of the U.S. population. Among the starkest findings is that 40% of respondents have attempted suicide in their lifetime—nearly nine times the attempted suicide rate in the U.S. population (4.6%). (National Center for Transgender Equality 2016, p.3)

This study highlights, first of all, the extremely damaging discrimination faced by transgender people, and secondly the added burden faced by transgender people of color. Looking at the areas of discrimination, one can surmise the additional hardships faced by transgender people of lesser financial means. Much of the support and relief transgender people seek requires accessing sophisticated medical care. Lack of insurance or lack of funds for services not covered by insurance is an oppressive limitation for transgender youth and their families. It can lead to hopelessness about getting the help they need.

INTERSECTIONALITY

Intersectionality is the study of 'the relation between systems of oppression which construct our multiple identities' (Carastathis 2014, p.304). As we strive to help transgender youth in our clinical work, we need to keep in mind that the challenges they face vary greatly with differences in race, gender, socioeconomic class, geography, religious affiliation, physical ability and disability, intellectual capabilities and so on. Certain family situations, such as frequent relocation or living in foster care, create additional challenges. The internet is an important source of support for trans teens today, and lack of access may create isolation and extra hardship. The existence, or not, of at least one supportive adult in a youth's life can make a tremendous difference in their ability to deal with the stresses and disadvantages discussed above. The incidence of these stressors varies greatly by community, sometimes by school within a given community, and certainly from family to family.

As clinicians we have to be prepared to assess a youth's needs, taking all of these domains into consideration. In particular we need to be cognizant of how these factors may limit a youth's access to validation, support and treatment. We cannot use a one-size-fits-all template that focuses solely on gender identity exploration in the therapy office. We must be ready to advocate for our clients in the contexts that are causing them distress, disadvantage and harassment. These may include family support, safety at school and access to medical services. All are affected by the multiple stigmatized identities mentioned above. We must keep in mind that trans people of color face much higher levels of violence and discrimination than their white peers. At the end of this chapter there is a list of memoirs reflecting the experiences of trans people from a wide range of backgrounds, as well as links to relevant videos.

HOMELESSNESS

The most vulnerable youth are those who are thrust into independence prematurely. Some teens are kicked out by their parents because they are transgender. Others leave home to escape abuse, or to seek a community they believe will be more supportive (Beam 2007; National Clearinghouse on Families and Youth 2016a). Among my clients, some hid their transgender identity after their parents, uncomfortable with their gender nonconformance, threatened that they would be beaten or kicked out if they were found out to be transgender. Others ended up in group homes or foster care after running away from parents who harassed them for being gender nonconforming or trans.

Among homeless youth in the United States, 40 percent identify as LGBTQ[1]. Most of them are youth of color (Keo-Meier and Hicks 2014). They are at risk of substance abuse, or turning to sex work to survive (Grossman and D'Augelli 2006; National Clearinghouse on Families and Youth 2016a). These practices increase their exposure to HIV, hepatitis and other diseases. Trans individuals who are unable to obtain medical care or unable to pay for it are more likely to seek illegal sources of hormones and take them without medical supervision (Meier and Labuski 2013). Some transfeminine people without access to care may self-inject with silicone to create or enhance feminine curves (Chyten-Brennan 2014). These are dangerous measures driven by desperate circumstances.

---

1   The 'Q' in LGBTQ usually refers to those who are questioning gender identity or sexual orientation.

Homeless youth are most likely to receive health, mental health and substance abuse services, if at all, at hospital clinics or LGBT-community health centers. Access to ongoing care is greatly enhanced by safe, long-term, trans-supportive housing. Without it, comprehensive health care and assistance with gender transition are unlikely to proceed optimally.

MICROAGGRESSION

Microaggression initially referred to 'brief and commonplace daily verbal, behavioral, and environmental indignities, whether intentional or unintentional, that communicate hostile, derogatory, or negative racial slights' (Sue *et al.* 2007, p.271). The definition has been expanded to include similar affronts toward other socially marginalized groups such as ethnic and sexual/gender minorities. Microaggressions toward transgender people include statements and behaviors that:

- are based on negative stereotypes about trans people
- suggest transgender identity is sick or sinful or wrong
- show discomfort with being around trans people
- assume all transgender people are the same
- deny there is discrimination against trans people.

Nonaffirmation, discussed in Chapter 2, is one form of micro-aggression trans people frequently encounter. Another is misgendering.

To *misgender* is to refer to someone by name, pronouns or gendered words (e.g., son, daughter) that do not fit with the individual's affirmed gender. Often this occurs when well-meaning individuals who knew someone prior to their affirmation of their trans identity use old language out of habit. This is understandable and easily remedied by a correction and an apology. Misgendering is aggressive when it is done in an intentional, hostile manner, and microaggressive when done casually with disregard for the statements or other indications the individual has presented regarding their affirmed gender. It is easy to underestimate the pain experienced by many transgender youth when they are misgendered. When this happens repeatedly, the young person may feel completely devalued, unsupported or invisible. Therapists and other trans community allies should exercise every effort to address people by their affirmed gender and name and with language that reflects their identity as female, male or of a non-binary gender. Gender-neutral words include person, child, student and attractive (vs. handsome or pretty). When in doubt about someone's gender identity, one can ask what their pronouns are if that seems appropriate and not intrusive in the situation, or one can stick to gender-neutral pronouns and language.

Microaggression against transgender people may take the form of language that suggests that they are not 'real' women or men, or by failing to include them in single-gender social groups or activities. And of course questioning a trans person's right to use the bathroom where they feel most comfortable is a form of microaggression that has been escalated in some areas of the United States to the passage of hostile legislation (Epps 2016).

RESPECT, INCLUSION AND AFFIRMATION

Therapists of transgender clients must start from a position of respect, inclusion and affirmation:

- Begin with the assumption that each individual is the authority on their gender identity.
- Ask for and honor the person's chosen name and pronouns, and be attentive to language.
- Accept that uncertainty can be part of the process of clarification, and that gender identity does not have to be proven to you or others.
- Understand that each person's gender identity is unique and does not have to fit an identified category or label.

Begin with the assumption that each individual is the authority on their gender identity

Sometimes therapists make the mistake of thinking their role is to determine a young person's correct gender identity and then guide them through the process of embracing it. While I will be talking in Chapter 6 about evaluating gender identity, this is not akin to evaluating a mental health condition. One's identity is not a mental health condition, despite the existence of a mental health diagnosis of 'Gender Dysphoria' in the American Psychiatric Association's current diagnostic manual (American Psychiatric Association 2013).

Evaluation of gender identity is the process of facilitating a discussion that allows the youth to talk about and reflect on various aspects of gender identity. While it also includes gathering information from the youth's parents when possible, the parents are not the final authorities on their child's gender identity. Your role is to provide an opportunity for the young person to do a thorough self-assessment in a safe and accepting environment, an environment that may not be easily available to them elsewhere. This will include open-ended discussion about their sense of self, gentle questioning about their experience of gender in their life so far, and suggestions for further exploration, which most likely will include trying out different gender expressions if they have not already done so. The evaluation is presented in detail in Chapter 6.

Ask for and honor the person's chosen name and pronouns, and be attentive to language

The best place to begin this process is with the paperwork clients fill out before their first session. Most likely, you need to have a space for the client's legal name. You may or may not need to include their birth-assigned sex. Your forms should definitely include a place for preferred name and if you ask for sex, also ask for gender identity. Leave a blank space here, rather than a list of choices. This should be on the registration form you use for all clients, not just those who have identified themselves in advance as transgender. In your first session with those who identify as transgender, queer or questioning, be sure to ask about preferred name and pronouns as well as who is aware of these, and whether it is safe or advisable to use them in front of the youth's parents.

In your private meetings with trans youth, keep in mind to always use their chosen name and pronouns. Ask them to correct you when you slip up, and always apologize and correct yourself when you do. Be cognizant of language that is gendered, as well as language that includes or excludes them from their affirmed gender cohort. For example, ask a trans boy how 'the other boys at school' are treating him, rather than how 'the boys' are treating him. The latter suggests he is not one of the boys.

Accept that uncertainty can be part of the process of clarification, and that gender identity does not have to be proven to you or others

For most transgender youth, their upbringing did not include early awareness that some people are transgender. In fact, they most likely received a multitude of messages from family, peers and the community that boys are boys, girls are girls, and those who differ from this order are devalued. So it is natural for transgender individuals to experience uncertainty as they come to understand and embrace their gender identity. It is important that you assure your teen and young adult clients that hearing their uncertainty does not cause you to doubt their ability to reach certainty about their gender identity.

Discussion in therapy as well as trying out different gender expressions when safe and possible are all part of the process of clarification. Clarity about gender identity is not required in advance. Uncertainty does not invalidate an individual's position as the authority on their own gender identity. Time spent embracing or affirming their birth-assigned gender may be part of this process of understanding who they are and does not cast doubt on their subsequently affirmed gender identity. In fact, for some youth, the experience of making a sincere effort to conform to their birth-assigned gender and being unhappy as a result gives them clarity about their actual gender identity and the courage to affirm it.

Understand that each person's gender identity is unique and does not have to fit an identified category or label

In *The Lives of Transgender People*, Beemyn and Rankin (2011) divide transgender individuals into four categories based on their assigned sex and affirmed gender identity: female-to-male/transgender (FTM/T), male-to-female/transgender (MTF/T), male-to-different-gender (MTDG), and female-to-different-gender (FTDG). The latter two categories are for those affirming non-binary identities. But as the study goes on to show, within these categories there is a great variety of individual difference.

Once you have gotten to know a significant number of transgender individuals, you will see that each trans person is unique. Knowing which of these categories they may fit into, or which labels they use to describe themselves, only gives you the bare outline of who they are. Awareness of their other affiliations and identities, as mentioned earlier in this chapter, gives you additional information. But the only way to truly understand a person's unique gender identity is to learn about it in detail from them. And the only way to know what will be their best course of action, should they feel the need to take action in the arena of gender transition, is to accompany them on that journey and learn as you go along.

FOR FURTHER EXPLORATION

Memoirs

Becoming a Visible Man, by Jamison Green, Vanderbilt University Press, 2004.

Gender Outlaw: On Men, Women and the Rest of Us, by Kate Bornstein, Vintage Books, 1994.

Just Add Hormones: An Insider's Guide to the Transsexual Experience, by Matt Kailey, Beacon Press, 2005.

Nina Here Nor There: My Journey Beyond Gender, by Nick Krieger, Beacon Press, 2011.

Redefining Realness: My Path to Womanhood, Identity, Love and So Much More, by Janet Mock, Atria Books, 2014.

Revolutionary Voices: A Multicultural Queer Youth Anthology, edited by Amy Sonnie, Alyson Publications, 2000.

Second Son: Transitioning Toward My Destiny, Love and Life, by Ryan K. Sallans, Title Town Publishing, 2012.

She's Not There: A Life in Two Genders, by Jennifer Finney Boylan, Broadway Books, 2003.

The Testosterone Files: My Hormonal and Social Transformation from FEMALE to MALE, by Max Wolf Valerio, Seal Press, 2006.

Transitioning Together: One Couple's Journey of Gender and Identity Discovery, by Wenn and Beatrice Lawson, Jessica Kingsley Publishers, 2017.

Transparent: Love, Family, and Living the T with Transgender Teenagers, by Cris Beam, Harcourt, Inc., 2007.

Whipping Girl: A Transsexual Woman on Sexism and the Scapegoating of Femininity, by Julia Serano, Seal Press, 2007.

Blogs and video

'10 Things You're Actually Saying When You Ignore Someone's Gender Pronouns' is from the 'Let's Queer Things Up!' blog, by Sam Dylan Finch. Available at www.everydayfeminism.com/2014/10/ignore-gender-pronouns

'That Guy Kas: Adventures of a Trans* Dude' is a blog. Available at https://thatguykas.wordpress.com

Trans People Speak is a collection of videos of a diverse group of trans people and their family and allies. Available at www.transpeoplespeak.org

DARKMATTER is a trans South Asian performance art duo comprising of Alok Vaid-Menon and Janani Balasubramanian. It is available at www.darkmatterpoetry.com. A video by Alok Vaid-Menon, part of the 'What's Underneath' series by Stylelikeu is available at www.stylelikeu.com/?s=alok

CHAPTER 5

Pathways to Transgender Identities

There are many different pathways to transgender awareness. Each transgender person's experience is unique. Julia Serano notes:

> People are used to hearing the canonical transsexual story of the person who knew ever since they were a child that they should have been the other gender, who subsequently struggled with those feelings for many years, until at some point they were finally able to transition to their identified gender, and then they lived happily ever after. Many transsexuals' experiences fit this general template, but others differ. Some people don't experience gender dysphoria and/or a desire to be the other gender until significantly later in their lives. Some happily live as members of a non-transsexual identity (e.g., crossdresser, genderqueer, gay or lesbian) for many years before coming to the understanding that they might be happier if they transition. Finally, transsexuals may differ in their social and physical transitions.[1] Many (such as myself) both socially and physically transition, while others may

---

1   Social transition is the step of living in one's affirmed gender either full time or in any social, family and community contexts where it is safe to do so. Physical transition refers to medical and non-medical interventions to change one's body to conform more fully to one's gender identity. These transition steps are discussed in Chapters 8–10.

be happy socially transitioning sans physical interventions. And others may physically transition but not fully socially transition (e.g., in cases where it is not safe for them to live full-time in their identified gender). (Serano 2016)

As you meet transgender or questioning teens in the clinical setting, keep in mind that each person's story is different and each one is valid. They are not required to have gained awareness of their transgender identity in a certain stepwise manner or at a certain age to be validated or supported. Your role is to help them increase self-understanding, sort through any confusion or doubts they have, address the impact of oppressive societal forces and gain the support they need from their families and their community. If you are able to accomplish this, then the next steps on their path, and what they need to maximize their well-being, will be reasonably clear.

GENDER NONCONFORMING CHILDREN

Every culture has its own expectations for male and female behaviors and interests. In the United States, for example, girls are expected to be emotional, demure and kind, play with dolls and enjoy clothes that are frilly and pastel-colored. Boys are expected to be stoic, rambunctious, more aggressive than girls and to frown on domestic activities. Each culture, in addition, allows a certain amount of latitude within which behavior that strays from the norm is accepted. Gender conforming children are those whose behaviors and interests fit reasonably well within the expectations of their culture. *Gender nonconforming* children are those whose behaviors and interests transgress cultural expectations for their sex.

Research suggests that if you follow a cohort of gender nonconforming children from early childhood into adulthood, only some of them will become transgender adults (Drescher and Pula 2014; Wallien and Cohen-Kettenis 2008). Thomas Steensma and his colleagues followed 127 children referred to a Gender Dysphoria clinic in Amsterdam, comparing those who persisted in their cross-gender identification with those who did not. They found that the 'persisters reported higher intensities of GD [gender dysphoria], more body dissatisfaction,' and children who stated they 'were' a boy or girl, rather than 'wishing they were,' were more likely to persist (Steensma *et al.* 2013, p.587). Ehrensaft found, in addition, that persisters approached gender exploration as 'serious work' rather than play (2016, p.61).

Practitioners of affirmative approaches to helping children who express a transgender identity advocate for early transition when a child is clamoring for it (Hidalgo *et al.* 2013). According to Ehrensaft:

> The child who implores the world to listen to his or her pleas that the world has gotten it wrong and he or she is in the wrong gender or the child who is not allowed to express gender in the way that feels right to him or her often shows signs of stress, distress, or behavioral disruption. Once allowed to transition, these children typically relax and the signs of stress, distress, and disruption dissipate, if not disappear altogether. (Ehrensaft 2012, p.346)

> To date, we have no research studies that indicate that a child who transitions gender and later transitions back in a gender fluid process rather than a frenzy of gender chaos or confusion suffers any damage to his or her psyche, and my own clinical observations are that such a process does indeed occur with no harm if the surrounding environment is accepting of the changes. (Ehrensaft 2012, p.354)

EARLY AWARENESS

Most transgender people report an early awareness of gender difference (Beemyn and Rankin 2011). The most commonly presented narrative for transgender teens is, similarly, very early awareness that their gender identity differs from what others expect, and a long and challenging struggle to be authentic (Jennings 2016; Kuklin 2014; Nutt 2015). In these instances the child is strongly gender nonconforming in ways that are easily visible to others. Many of these children express, at least once, to one of their parents or guardians that their gender is different from their assigned sex. Many of these children and their families, in the ensuing years, suffer through conflict and distress before they reach acceptance and happiness.

Young people who express their gender identity emphatically at an early age and have enough family and community support to live in their affirmed gender have generally reached certainty about this by the time they enter puberty. Puberty may exacerbate their distress about the discordance between their body and their inner self (Beemyn and Rankin 2011; Brill and Pepper 2008; Ehrensaft 2011). Having made the transition to living in their affirmed gender before puberty, they are able to take advantage of medical interventions that allow them to have a puberty roughly in sync with their same-gender peers, and they are able to avoid the pubertal masculinization or feminization of their bodies that is incorrect for their gender identity.

As I mentioned earlier, narratives about this path to transgender identity prevail in the media. As a result, this may be what clinicians come to expect when they first encounter a transgender client. Unfortunately, this can lead to a devaluation of the significance of other pathways and an invalidation of those whose journey looks different.

AWARENESS AT PUBERTY

For about 40 percent of the teens I have worked with, the discordance was not as obvious to them in childhood and was not visible to others. They may have experienced a sense of being different from other kids but had no clarity about that difference. They tended to fit in relatively easily with their peers of the same assigned sex. Their parents viewed them as relatively typical girls or boys. There were no arguments about what they would wear or do or what toys they would play with or who they would play with. Similarly, Grossman and D'Augelli (2006) found that most of the transgender teens in their study became aware that their gender did not correspond to their birth-assigned sex around the onset of puberty.

It is easy to understand why puberty is the time that many transgender youth come to awareness. As their body begins to change in a clear feminine or masculine direction, they have a strong visceral sense that these changes are wrong for them. They are disturbed by what they see reflected back to them in the mirror. They seek information. Once they find out about transgender identities, they have words to describe who they are. They discover they are not the only ones who feel this way.

For the parents of these teens, the declaration of transgender identity seems to come completely out of the blue. It is very difficult for these parents to give credence initially to what their child is saying. Katie Rain Hill reminds us that the only authority on a person's gender identity is that individual:

> I want to be clear that my love of stereotypical girl toys...is not what makes me female... What makes me female is something I felt in the core of myself: that my external body did not match up with how I felt inside, and that I was being seen by others as something I was not. (Hill 2014, p.44)

Those whose awareness emerges at puberty often have a sense of playing catch-up. They become alarmed about their birth-assigned sex at a time when their body is already changing. They may have difficulty gaining rapid recognition and support from their parents. Medical interventions require a number of preparatory steps: self-awareness; acknowledgment to others; access to medical care; and in most instances, evaluation and referral by a mental health professional. These steps, in the best of circumstances, create a delay that is highly distressing to many transgender teens. When family and professional support is not readily available, the delay can seem endless, leaving the youth without hope of relief from their distress.

Teens who begin their social transition in adolescence have to manage this on top of the social challenges that all teenagers experience: figuring out where they fit in, their aspirations and goals and their value to themselves and others. Supportive peers and adults are crucial to the success of this project. The responses of friends, acquaintances at school, parents, teachers and others in the community will have a tremendous impact on whether the teen thrives.

LATER AWARENESS

Beemyn and Rankin (2011) report that the majority of their respondents felt uncertain about their assigned gender before age 13, but they may not yet have had the words to describe how they felt. Those coming into full awareness in their late teen or young adult years have generally completed most or all of the physical changes of puberty. Those whose sexual attractions are toward those of their same assigned sex may have considered their identity to be lesbian or gay until they realized their gender was different. Or they may have embraced 'bisexual' as a label that somehow approximated who they were.

Those who come to their transgender awareness well past the onset of puberty are likely to be distressed about the physical changes that have already occurred. Many feel a great urgency to live in their affirmed gender as soon as possible. They may be anxious to pursue medical intervention, and face the same delays mentioned above. They may also feel despair about having missed out on puberty blockers, and envy those with early awareness and family support. Meier and Labuski note:

> There is no single or correct trans history or identity, as the population is more diverse than most imagine. There are some people whose gender identity is fluid and changes over time,

others report feeling 'trapped in the wrong body' since early childhood, still others do not discover their gender identity until late in life. (2013, p.314)

For those who make a binary transition well into or past puberty, the discordance between their body characteristics and their gender identity is more likely to be evident to others. They may experience a high level of stress if they are frequently seen as transgender by strangers and have no way of knowing how they will be treated. They are at risk of being accosted for using a public restroom. They may, in fact, experience hostility from others in whatever restroom they use if their gender presentation does not conform fully to societal expectations of either sex.

NON-BINARY PATHWAYS

Non-binary pathways can be the most confusing for cisgender clinicians to understand. We are raised to think of gender as falling into only two boxes, and some of our mental health training delves specifically into differences based on two gender categories. Girls are found to be more prone to eating disorders and acts of self-harm, while boys are more likely to have Attention Deficit Hyperactivity Disorder (ADHD) or anger management problems. The discussion takes place in a world where a child is either a girl or a boy. There are no other options. As a result, it is easier for many of us to understand that someone could affirm the opposite gender, than to understand what it means to affirm neither gender, or both, or something completely different. Throughout this book I will discuss the particular challenges faced by non-binary youth and their families, to help broaden your understanding of transgender youth and how to help them. As with those who transition in the binary sense, those who transition to non-binary identities include youth who were gender nonconforming as children as well as those who fit in easily enough with societal gender expectations.

Here is how Reid Vanderburgh, who transitioned from female to not-female, describes the experience of non-binary gender before gaining clarity about it:

> I'd never had conscious fantasies about being male. I had just never felt completely at home in my skin as a female, causing a low-grade anxiety and depression that was growing steadily as I aged. I hated women's bathrooms. I did not like introducing myself to others, as my former name was highly feminine. I avoided describing myself as a lesbian, and felt vaguely uncomfortable referring to myself as a woman. I had never visited an ob/gyn in my life. I was full of contradictions and felt like an enigma to myself. (Vanderburgh 2001, p.26)

FOR FURTHER EXPLORATION

Teen memoirs

Being Jazz: My Life as a (Transgender) Teen, by Jazz Jennings, Crown Books for Young Readers, 2016.

Beyond Magenta: Transgender Teens Speak Out, by Susan Kuklin, Candlewick Press, 2014.

Rethinking Normal: A Memoir in Transition, by Katie Rain Hill, Simon and Schuster, 2014.

Some Assembly Required: The Not-So-Secret Life of a Transgender Teen, by Arin Andrews, Simon and Schuster, 2014.

Articles and books

'Between pink and blue: A multi-dimensional family approach to gender nonconforming children and their families,' by Jean Malpas, *Family Process 50*, 4, 453–70, 2011.

The Conscious Parent's Guide to Gender Identity: A Mindful Approach to Embracing Your Child's Authentic Self, by Darlene Tando, Adams Media, 2016.

'Desisting and persisting gender dysphoria after childhood: A qualitative follow-up study,' by Thomas Steensma *et al.*, *Clinical Child Psychology and Psychiatry 16*, 4, 499–516, 2011.

The Gender Creative Child: Pathways for Nurturing and Supporting Children Who Live Outside Gender Boxes, by Diane Ehrensaft, The Experiment, 2016.

The Transgender Child: A Handbook for Families and Professionals, by Stephanie Brill and Rachel Pepper, Cleis Press, 2008.

'Transgender kids: What does it take to help them thrive?' by Francine Russo, *Scientific American Mind 27,* 1, 26–35, 2016.

Videos

'Becoming Me,' episode 2107 of *In the Life*. Search for this title at www.cinema. ucla.edu

'Jacob's Journey: Raising a Transgender Child.' Search for this title at www. nbcnews.com

ASSESSMENT

CHAPTER 6

Evaluation of Gender Identity

The evaluation is a shared exploration of the young person's gender identity by the youth, the clinician and, ideally, the parents. Together we are seeking to find out if there has been a clear and persistent awareness of transgender identity. We are also evaluating whether a social transition would be safe, helpful for the young person's well-being, and further the process of clarifying their gender identity. In most cases we are also contemplating whether medical intervention is best for this individual. Generally the question of medical intervention is raised initially by the youth, but in some instances it may be a parent or a mental health clinician who brings this question to the table if they feel it is in the young person's best interest to consider it.

In my experience this exploration needs to encompass at least the following four topics:

- sense of self
- group affiliation
- body discomfort
- regard by others.

Each of these factors is viewed through a historical lens, to see which have persisted, what doubts the individual harbors, and how they have handled disclosure to others. We look as well at the youth's information-gathering, expression of gender and expectations for gender transition.

SENSE OF SELF

'It's just who I am.'
'I've always been a girl.'
'I'm a boy, that's all.'
'I never felt like a boy *or* a girl.'

If you are cisgender you most likely never wondered if you were male, female, neither or both. What others told you most likely fits your inner sense of who you are. So it can be difficult to grasp the simplicity and clarity of a teenager's certainty about a gender identity that does not conform to their assigned sex. If asked, you might find it difficult to explain how you are certain of your own gender. It's just something that seems to be true and it fits with the messages you have received from others throughout your life. Those who have not received external validation for the gender they feel themselves to be inside may also have very little to say about how they know their gender. And those with non-binary identities may have previously been completely without words to express who they are. Gender identity is an inner sense of self. A person may be sure of this without really being able to explain much about it. For that reason, we look into the other factors discussed below as well as the history of this awareness and the expectations that come with it.

Many of the clinicians who work extensively with young children emphasize that those who are likely to persist in their transgender identity will say, 'I am a boy' or 'I am a girl,' whereas those who say 'I wish I were' are less likely to persist in affirming a transgender identity (Ehrensaft 2016; Steensma *et al.* 2011). In my experience, teenagers reflecting on their childhood use the language of desire as often as they use the language of identity. They will typically say, 'I always wished I was a girl' or 'I wished I could become a girl' or 'I prayed that when I woke up in the morning I would be a boy.' So I caution against applying this language standard when taking a teen's history, or even when considering their initial statements early in the evaluation. By the time they reach their teenage years they may have learned again and again that they cannot be who they know themselves to be inside so they speak in terms of wishing they were that person.

While many of the teens who came to see me were certain they were transgender, there were a number of natal boys, 12–13 years old, who were highly uncertain. They said they 'wanted to be' a girl and were distressed about the onset of puberty, but they expressed confusion about whether they wanted to make a social transition or consider medical intervention in the future. Along with distress about their current state of being, they felt overwhelmed about what might be involved in a social transition. They felt uncertain about whether they would benefit from medical intervention. They each had a range of interests and sometimes a manner that were considered feminine in our culture. They were attracted to boys, rather than to girls as was culturally expected for natal boys. Some had considered female names. Some were interested in puberty blockers.

For each of these youths, the evaluation included discussion of how they viewed their gender, in what ways they were uncomfortable about being a boy, in what ways they would be more comfortable living as a girl, how they envisioned the process of gender transition for them, how they thought others would react, and so on. While each youth began with the language of wanting to be a girl rather than saying, 'I am a girl,' over time it became clear that some of these teens felt that they needed to live as girls. These were the ones who became excited about the prospect of a social transition and began to feel as well some urgency about beginning hormone treatment. The social transition experience for them turned out to be confirming of their female gender identity. Once transition was well underway, they were certain it was the right path for them. Their subsequent transition with hormones was affirming as well.

For the others, it took a few months to a year of therapy for them to clarify that they did not want a gender transition. They knew that if they had been girls, their interests, manner and attractions to boys would not be considered problematic. They would be girls with feminine interests who were attracted to boys. They would be easily accepted by their peers and their community. But they also realized that they were not girls. They were feminine gay or bisexual boys. Some wondered if they might have a non-binary gender identity, but not to the extent that they needed to do anything about it or ask people to address them differently.

It is important to note that in most of these cases the parents accepted fairly early on that their child might be transgender and were open to discussion about possible transition steps. They had brought their children to see me because I was known to be a therapist who worked with transgender youth in a supportive manner. The different outcomes for these teenagers were not based on the responses of their parents or the likely reactions they would have received at school. The difference was in how they felt inside, which became clear through discussion of their inner sense of self and the additional factors discussed in the rest of this chapter.

And how do young people with non-binary identities describe who they are? Their inner sense of self is neither female nor male, or it may be a blend of the two. Youth who are aware of non-binary terminology are apt to use terms such as the ones listed in Chapter 3. Some use different terms at different times. Their identities may be in flux and the terms are imprecise. Young people who enter therapy when they are just beginning to sort things out, and who have not yet heard these terms, may describe themselves in a variety of ways. Some of the descriptors my clients have used are 'more girl than boy,' 'not a girl and not a boy,' 'just not male' (for someone assigned male at birth), 'not female' (for someone assigned female at birth) and 'crossdresser with ambiguous gender.' One of the teens in *Beyond Magenta* states, 'But I like to be recognized as not a boy and not a girl. I'm gender queer, gender fluid, and gender other' (Kuklin 2014, p.96). Testa, Coolhart and Peta (2015, p.23) offer the following example of non-binary youth experience: 'I never really felt like a boy, but I never really felt like a girl either. I just wish I could move somewhere that gender doesn't exist and be me – not a boy or a girl.'

For those with uncertain or non-binary gender identities, evaluating how they feel when experiencing themselves in different gender presentations helps clarify their inner sense of self. If the process of trying out more masculine or feminine presentation leads to being viewed by others as the gender opposite their assigned sex, rather than as in-between, they have a chance to sense what a binary gender transition might be like. Keep in mind that each person's path is unique.

GROUP AFFILIATION

One indicator of discordant gender identity in children is their strong wish to affiliate with peers of their affirmed gender rather than with peers of their assigned sex (Cohen-Kettenis and Pfäfflin 2003). This generally includes an affinity for the activities that are more typically engaged in by those of their affirmed gender, and a deep sense of disappointment when they are excluded from those activities. For these children the schoolroom practice of boys lining up on one side of the room and girls lining up on the other side of the room is problematic. They may be deeply wounded when they receive the message from their peers, 'no girls allowed' or 'no boys.' Many transgender youth report these kinds of feelings in childhood.

In keeping with our understanding that there are many pathways to transgender identity, we find that other transgender teens did not experience this yearning in childhood. They may not have had a strong sense of gender identity or gender affiliation growing up. Rather they felt free to be who they were without much concern about gender and to participate in whatever activities and with whatever peers they preferred. For them, affiliation did not become an issue until the onset of puberty.

For teens in middle school,[1] and with the onset of puberty, gender segregation manifests itself in a more pronounced way than it had in the latency years. This can be a painful time for all LGBT youth as typically their peers are hanging out in same-sex groups and talking about their interest in the opposite sex. Adolescence is a time of increased interest in peer relationships and a diminished focus on family, so being unable to fit in with peers is especially disappointing. For some transgender teens, the yearning to be accepted as part of a gendered peer group is intense. For others, finding a peer group that is unconcerned about gender is most important.

BODY DISCOMFORT

Many trans people feel a strong discordance between their physiology and their gender identity. This body discomfort may be present in childhood or may emerge in puberty. Body discomfort related to gender identity is focused on gendered parts of the body. There may be a sense of having the wrong genitalia, beginning in childhood or later, or discomfort with secondary sex characteristics in puberty. Some youths disassociate themselves from these gendered body parts. Arin Andrews recalls his experience of showering, 'numb as usual to my breasts, aware of them only as objects, something external to run soap over' (2014, p.49). When trans people explore sexual intimacy, many inform their partners that certain parts of their bodies are off-limits or only to be touched in certain ways, for reasons of gender discordance (Hill-Meyer and Scarborough 2014).

Distress about actual or impending changes in puberty causes many transgender teens to be impatient about initiating hormone treatment – delay may bring pronounced and irreversible changes. As part of the gender identity evaluation, it is helpful to engage the youth in discussion of their body discomfort. It is important to

---

1   Middle school students in the United States range in age from approximately 11 to 14 years old.

understand whether physiology is a major concern for this youth, and especially if they have a sense of desperation about it that puts them in danger of self-harm. Parents and other adults may make statements that are well intended but ultimately dismissive such as, 'At your age I was uncomfortable with the ways my body was changing, too.' Body discomfort is a real and often highly significant aspect of a transgender youth's distress. Dismissive statements may lead the youth to feel unsupported and hopeless. These feelings in turn create a greater risk of self-harm, either from despair or as a way to be taken seriously.

This aspect of the assessment also informs the relevance and timing of referrals for medical intervention. Early in the evaluation there may be some confusion about whether a youth's body discomfort is related to gender identity or is a manifestation of something else, such as an eating disorder or autism spectrum disorders. Sorting out these and other mental health questions is discussed in Chapter 7.

REGARD BY OTHERS

Self-esteem depends on receiving positive feedback from others. The person who is self-assured enough to truly not care what other people think most likely had a good deal of support and affirmation earlier in life, creating a solid sense of self-confidence. Most LGBT teens are struggling to some degree with whether they can be respected by others in their authentic public presentation. That challenge has become significantly easier for lesbian, gay and bisexual (LGB) youth over the last two decades, but it is still a tremendous struggle for some. Social pressures to conform to gender roles and expectations are particularly strong in early adolescence. Thus, 'while the dramatic social changes in the last decades have led to unprecedented possibilities for LGBTQ youth to come out, the argument that risk is no longer relevant in their lives ignores their interpersonal and cultural realities' (Russell 2010, p.5).

Validation by peers can be particularly difficult for teen boys whose appearance does not fit the cultural norm (Horn and Romeo 2010).

When I speak of the importance of regard by others, and how that fits into the evaluation of transgender identity, I am referring primarily to the individual's desire to be accepted and embraced in their affirmed gender identity. Most often a young trans person will first disclose their identity or the fact that they are questioning gender identity to a friend or two. The kids I have worked with were able to figure out reasonably well in advance which friends would be open-minded and supportive. They were rarely disappointed in the response. The most common was a nonchalant 'OK' and shrug of the shoulders that was perfectly fine for the transgender youth: the new information was understood and then they were on to their next adventure.

Disclosure to parents was generally higher risk, as the home environment and family support were at stake. And the youths' ability to predict their parents' response was less accurate. Many were surprised that parents who were comfortable when they came out earlier as gay or lesbian were upset with the disclosure of a trans identity. While it is true that parents who were antagonistic to LGB identities were likely to be antagonistic to transgender identity (and thus less likely to have their teen disclose this to them), it was not true that parents at ease with gay and lesbian people would embrace their transgender child without doubt or alarm.

Once the initial disclosures are past, regard refers to the importance of others honoring a youth's choice of name and pronouns, using appropriately gendered language and including the youth in gendered groupings that fit their affirmed gender. The extent to which affirmation by others is important varies from youth to youth. As with body discomfort, understanding this aspect of the youth's gender identity helps us in planning for the youth – in this case for the social transition. Figuring out how this youth will advocate for themself, how much intervention they need or want in this effort from supportive adults and how much distress they are experiencing when they are misgendered are all intrinsic to supporting the young person's well-being.

HISTORY

It is useful to ascertain when and to what degree of intensity the individual has experienced these various aspects of gender identity awareness. This allows for a deeper understanding of the youth's gender, and hopefully is useful for the young person as well to deepen self-understanding. The history is not for the purpose of judging whether the young person's transgender identity is 'real.' It is simply an examination of how the person's gender identity has evolved over time. Gender identity awareness is a process of early certainty for some and gradual certainty for others. The value of examining the history of gender awareness is to help the young person achieve as much clarity as possible about who they are and how they would like to proceed. For those under 18, the evaluation also serves to reassure the parents that someone with gender identity expertise has helped their child carry out a thorough self-investigation so that any future steps taken are based on a solid foundation.

As we look over the history together, including discussion with parents of their awareness of gender nonconforming behaviors, preferences and expressions, there are a number of important aspects to consider:

- *Persistence:* Has there been a steady expression of gender nonconformance or transgender identity for a number of months or years? Have these feelings varied in intensity or disappeared altogether at times?
- *Doubts:* Has the child felt free to express doubts without those being used by others to undermine their self-confidence about gender identity and expression?
- *Disclosures:* When and to whom has the young person disclosed their transgender identity? Have they been afraid

to disclose? How did they feel about positive and negative responses they received?

- *Information-gathering:* Has the youth spent time gathering information, usually on the internet, about gender identity? Have they watched videos of other youth expressing transgender identity or documenting their transition? Have these viewings confirmed for them that what they are feeling is similar to other trans youth?
- *Expression:* Has the young person had the support and safety to try out different gender expressions? If so, have they done so? What have they learned about themselves from these experiences, both in how they felt intrinsically and how they felt about the affirming or unsupportive responses from others?
- *Expectations:* Does the youth have a realistic sense of what they may experience as they transition to their affirmed gender? If they have learned about the experiences of others, have these other individuals faced challenges this youth is likely to encounter? Do they understand what medical interventions do and do not change? Are they prepared to manage the range of reactions they may receive from others? Do they have supports in place in advance to assist them if any difficulties arise?

SOCIAL TRANSITION

The social transition is most often the first step in gender transition, and at the same time it can serve as part of the gender identity evaluation, especially for youth. Social transition is when the young person begins to live in their affirmed gender, either full time or in any social, family and community contexts where it is safe to do so. This may include any or all of the following: requesting that others address them by a different name and set of pronouns; changing their clothing, hairstyle, jewelry or makeup; altering their voice; and affiliating with groups and activities associated with their affirmed gender. For teens, school is the most important social context.

Some teens and young adults make a social transition before seeking therapy. For some, it happens in conjunction with their exploration of gender in therapy. The social transition generally brings greater clarity about gender identity, or confirmation for those who are already clear about who they are; they find that they are happier living in their affirmed gender, even with the built-in challenges, than they are conforming to their assigned sex. For this reason I am a strong advocate of social transition whenever it is desired by the youth and safe to do so. If it is desired and not safe, emotionally or otherwise, I advocate creating or finding safe spaces to express their authentic self, even if only part time. If it turns out after social transition that the school environment is unsafe, a family will have to seek a new school environment or, in extreme cases, relocate for the well-being of the child (see for example, Nutt 2015).

For parents, observing how their children fare once they are able to live more authentically is usually reassuring, as they see the acceptance their child receives (which is often better than the parents expected), how the young person handles the challenges that arise, and their overall demeanor once they are free to be themselves. The social transition could on the other hand turn out to be an experience that causes a youth to doubt or decide against going ahead with irreversible transition steps such as medical interventions, but in my experience this has not been the case. Sometimes the social transition has clarified a slightly different understanding of their transgender identity, but I have not known anyone whose social transition convinced them they are actually cisgender.

CONCLUDING THE EVALUATION

The goal of the evaluation is for the youth to reach a relatively clear sense of who they are, with a significant degree of comfort and certainty. For each person, some of the factors listed above turn out to be more important than others. The only element present for all trans youth is that their sense of self is other than the gender corresponding to their assigned sex. No single other factor is needed to 'prove' they are transgender, and of course they should not have to prove this to anyone but themselves. The breadth of the evaluation is to establish a more complex and coherent idea of who they are, given that they have usually grown up without a natural process of open-ended identity exploration. So many doors were closed to them along the way.

For those 18 years and older, I see the evaluator in a consulting role, conducting the evaluation to the extent that the young person finds it helpful; ruling out severe mental health problems, such as active psychosis, that could at least temporarily render someone unable to decide on medical interventions; and assisting the young person in accessing the resources for whatever transition steps they feel are right for them.

For those under 18, however, clinicians are expected to advise the young person and their parents or guardians about the value of social transition, their readiness for medical intervention and the possible benefits and risks of these steps. Parents, who will have to be prepared to support the youth through the challenges of a social transition and whose assent is needed for treatment, are relying on the clinician to give them assurance that these steps are necessary for their child's well-being.

FOR FURTHER EXPLORATION

Books and articles

Artistic Expressions of Transgender Youth, by Tony Ferraiolo, Tony Ferraiolo, LLC, 2015.

'Ethical, legal, and psychosocial issues in care of transgender adolescents,' by Catherine Holman and Joshua Goldberg, *International Journal of Transgenderism* 9, 3/4, 95–110, 2006.

'Gender trajectories: Transsexual people coming to terms with their gender identities,' by Nuno Pinto and Carla Moleiro. *Professional Psychology: Research and Practice 46*, 1, 12–20, 2015.

The Lives of Transgender People, by Genny Beemyn and Susan Rankin, Columbia University Press, 2011.

'Therapy with transsexual youth and their families: A clinical tool for assessing youth's readiness for gender transition,' by Deborah Coolheart *et al., Journal of Marital and Family Therapy 39*, 2, 223–43, 2013.

Transgender Emergence: Therapeutic Guidelines for Working with Gender-Variant People and Their Families, by Arlene Istar Lev, Haworth Clinical Practice Press, 2004.

Transgenderism and Intersexuality in Childhood and Adolescence: Making Choices, by Peggy Cohen-Kettenis and Friedemann Pfafflin, Sage Publications, 2003.

CHAPTER 7

Transgender Identities and Mental Health

Assessment and treatment of mental health problems are essential aspects of psychotherapy for all clients. Transgender youth are no exception. Disclosure of transgender identity may occur prior to the start of therapy, and may be the sole reason the individual or family is seeking counseling. Awareness or questioning of gender identity may occur in the course of psychotherapy that was initiated to address a mental health problem without any mention of gender identity concerns at the start. A client may enter therapy with both significant mental health concerns and concerns about gender identity. For transgender teens, it is often the case that the teen is seeking help solely for gender transition while the family views the teen as suffering from a mental health problem.

Each of these scenarios leads to a different sequencing of mental health assessment and gender identity evaluation. The severity of any concurrent mental health problem dictates further how the treatment proceeds. Severe mental illness will have an impact on the pacing of whatever transition steps are determined to be appropriate for the youth, especially steps involving irreversible medical interventions. The individual's level of distress about gender discordance is also a factor in the speed and sequencing of transition steps. As an identified gender identity specialist, I have often provided consultation for youth who were already in treatment with another therapist for months or years before gender identity was discussed. In those cases I provided a gender identity evaluation, family therapy and consultation with the other therapist, who continued to treat the youth during and after my work with them.

The key to working with clients with a stigmatized identity, including LGBT people and members of other oppressed groups, is to remain cognizant of the impact of stigma on the individual, in the present as well as in their past. Hendricks and Testa write:

> Trans people, like the general population, have general life stressors that may result in a wide range of reasons for presenting to a psychologist for care. However, on top of general life stressors, trans people are subjected to alarmingly high rates of discrimination, violence, and rejection related to their gender identity or expression. We understand the higher prevalence of mental disorders in trans individuals to be related to these experiences. This is consistent with the parallel work of Meyer (2003), who proposed that the higher incidence of mental disorders found among lesbian, gay and bisexual (LGB) people, was essentially the result of a 'hostile and stressful social environment' (p. 674) to which LGB people are subjected as a result of their sexual minority status. (Hendricks and Testa 2012, p.462)

The gender identity evaluation is the cornerstone of clinical work with transgender youth. When the evaluation is conducted in a supportive manner, it serves to help the young person clarify their gender identity and determine appropriate and necessary transition steps. Receiving support and carrying out transition steps generally relieves some of the distress the young person has been experiencing. While I will discuss transition steps in detail in Chapters 8 and 9, suffice it to say here that these steps initially include disclosure to significant others (especially parents and friends) followed by opportunities for outward expression of authentic gender. Therapy can be the setting for sorting out who needs to know, how to disclose safely, and how to manage any negative responses.

Therapists working with transgender teens will also need to advocate directly for their clients, perhaps in a way they have not routinely done with other teen clients. This includes family therapy and either contact with the school or coaching the teen and family about their interactions with the school. Changes at home and at school bring the youth additional relief from distress. For some this relief leads to joy about being free to be oneself and getting validation by others. If distress does not diminish, the process needs closer examination: either these are not appropriate steps for this youth or else the environment is too hostile for them to carry out their transition in a safe and healthy way. One aspect or the other needs further attention.

Those of us who provide affirming mental health care for transgender youth do not view transgender identity itself as a mental health condition or illness. Yet we have to include 'Gender Dysphoria' as a mental health diagnosis when supporting these youth in accessing medical treatments they need for gender transition. I'll begin with a look at the diagnosis of Gender Dysphoria, and then go on to discuss specific mental health symptoms and conditions that may be present for a youth who is seeking counseling for transgender identity concerns.

DOES GENDER DYSPHORIA BELONG AS A MENTAL HEALTH DIAGNOSIS?

In considering this question it is instructive to look at the diagnostic shift in relation to our understanding of same-sex love. Prior to 1973, 'Homosexuality' was an illness in the American Psychiatric Association's *Diagnostic and Statistical Manual of Mental Disorders (DSM)*. Same-sex feelings and behavior were understood to be dysfunctional and stunted variants of heterosexuality. There were various theories as to what caused this and how to 'cure' it. Irving Bieber, a psychiatrist who was a leader in the view of homosexuality as a mental illness, believed that 'fears and inhibitions associated with heterosexuality are circumvented and sexual responsivity with pleasure and excitement to a member of the same sex develops as a pathologic alternative' (Bieber *et al.* 1962, p.303). This is very different from our current understanding of same-sex attraction as a natural variation in sexual orientation.

In 1973, after protests about this diagnosis alongside a growing public awareness of well-functioning gay and lesbian people, the diagnosis was changed to 'Ego-Dystonic Homosexuality.' This diagnosis suggested that while not all homosexual people were mentally ill, those who felt ashamed and uncomfortable about being gay or lesbian had a mental illness. It was impossible for any adult in 1973 to have grown up in an environment of acceptance and support of their same-sex orientation. As a result, most of us had some degree of internalized shame or self-denigration to deal with. Pathologizing this natural response to societal oppression (and some of the secretive self-protecting behaviors that resulted) was also wrong, and in 1987 this diagnosis was removed altogether (Lev 2004).

Looking back on the history of diagnoses pathologizing lesbian, gay and bisexual people, whose sexual orientations differed from what our culture expected, we can see that we are in the midst of the same process for the diagnoses applied to transgender people, whose gender identities differ from societal expectations. Prior to the most recent *DSM*, the diagnosis of 'Gender Identity Disorder' (GID) designated trans people as having a mental illness. The criteria for the illness included many characteristics typical of transgender people, such as identifying with a gender that does not conform to one's assigned sex and desiring to live in that gender (American Psychiatric Association 2000).

Thus, transgender identity was considered an illness, and the natural expression of that identity along with the desires and feelings typically experienced by trans people were the symptoms of that illness (Butler 2006). Non-binary identities were not addressed.

Activists involved in the writing of the latest *DSM* (American Psychiatric Association 2013) were able to secure the replacement of GID with Gender Dysphoria. Gender Dysphoria is described as a feeling of sadness or distress caused by the discordance between a person's assigned sex and their gender identity or expression. According to *DSM-5*, when Gender Dysphoria is used as a mental health diagnosis for teens and adults, it requires at least six months of feeling this discordance and experiencing distress or impairment as a result. The diagnosis again lists feelings, desires and beliefs typical of many trans people. This version includes those with non-binary identities.

This diagnosis, while no longer titled a 'disorder,' still pathologizes the common experiences of transgender people. It also suggests that transgender people seeking medical services have 'clinically significant' distress or impairment. This assumption disregards those who are functioning well and have a positive view of their identity and their life possibilities. There is little explication in the *DSM* of the fact that the distress or impairment can be a result of societal forces rather than an internal matter. In these ways this diagnosis resembles Ego-Dystonic Homosexuality as the last holdout of a health system that is not able to see transgender identities as normal variations of human existence. Were it not for one caveat, those advocating for the change in diagnosis would have aimed to remove the mental health diagnosis altogether, rather than simply revamping it with less offensive and more inclusive language (Lev 2004; Winters 2008).

The caveat is that as of now the Gender Dysphoria diagnosis is the only available medical justification for hormone treatment and for gender affirmation surgeries. Physicians who provide these treatments and insurers who pay for them need the diagnosis to validate medical necessity for those trans people who want and need them. My view is that the *International Classification of Diseases (ICD)*, which includes both medical and mental health diagnoses, should include a medical diagnosis indicating that an individual experiences a discordance between their physiology and their gender identity and as a result is requesting medical intervention to bring their physical being into greater congruence with their gender. 'Ultimately, replacing psychiatric diagnosis altogether with nomenclature of a physical medical condition has long been the goal of many trans-advocates concerned about twin issues of stigma and access to transition procedures' (Winters 2008, p.175). Once this is in place, there will be no need for a gender-identity-related diagnosis in the *DSM* (or the mental health portion of the *ICD*).

ADDRESSING MENTAL HEALTH PROBLEMS

According to Amy Tishelman and her colleagues:

> We know that transgender youth are at risk for anxiety, depression, self-harm, suicidal ideation, psychiatric hospitalizations, homelessness, exploitation, and abuse... In addition, the spectrum of issues that can present in any child or adolescent can present in gender variant youth, including history of trauma, oppositional defiant disorder or conduct disorder, and learning disabilities. (Tishelman *et al.* 2015, p.42)

My general paradigm for addressing mental health problems experienced by transgender youth is as follows:

1. Address the mental health problems in tandem with evaluating gender identity and supporting any appropriate transition steps. Appropriate steps are those that are desired by the trans youth, safe to undertake and likely to provide validation, relief from distress and/or further clarity about their gender identity.
2. For mild to moderate mental health symptoms, start with the expectation that the symptoms will reduce in intensity and frequency or disappear altogether as the youth's affirmed gender identity is understood, supported and actualized. If the young person instead experiences hurtful or hostile responses as this process unfolds, symptoms that are due

to stigma and oppression are likely to recur until these responses are addressed. Another risk factor for resurgence of symptoms is disappointment of expectations the youth has over how transition will proceed. This is one reason for including a discussion of expectations in the evaluation and continuing to discuss how the experience is meeting the youth's expectations, what major disappointments if any have occurred and how to improve or come to terms with these.

3. Youth with clearly diagnosed moderate to severe mental illness, and those with less severe symptoms that have not abated in supportive counseling and early transition, will most likely need treatment that is specific to these conditions in addition to validation and support for their gender identity.

4. Since a single mental health clinician cannot have subspecialties in all mental health areas, many youth need treatment from one or more other clinicians or programs in addition to the gender-focused counseling. When referring your client for ancillary care, you must find providers who are open-minded about transgender identities and do not see trans identity as a mental illness. Ideally these providers will be knowledgeable about gender identity and aware of the impact of negative societal responses on trans people, but you may find that you have to provide that information and perspective for other providers. Referrals may include evaluation for treatment with psychiatric medication, inpatient or intensive outpatient treatment, Dialectical Behavioral Therapy, and subspecialties such as eating disorders, trauma, dissociative disorders and substance abuse.

5. When gender identity concerns arise in the course of ongoing treatment for mental illness, continuing on two tracks is the best course. The mental health treatment continues and the gender identity evaluation begins. My experience with clients previously treated for mental illness is that some or all of the mental health symptoms diminished or disappeared as the gender concerns were addressed.

6. Often the young person's history includes one or more experiences of trauma or loss. Parents and clinicians may wonder if the expression of transgender identity is somehow a result of these occurrences. It is essential when taking a history to see whether these incidents precede or follow early awareness of gender difference. In many instances the disclosure of transgender identity came after the traumatic incident, but the history reveals that the awareness of gender difference preceded it. Whether or not the history suggests that the trauma, loss and gender identity are interrelated, clinicians must approach these issues in treating transgender youth as they would for cisgender youth with similar histories. While this question was raised a number of times in my practice by parents or other clinicians who had previously treated the child, there was not a single youth who at the onset of their work with me or after exploration in therapy concluded that trauma or loss had affected their sense of where their gender identity fell on the female to male spectrum.

SPECIFIC MENTAL HEALTH CONDITIONS

For the rest of this chapter I will focus on the specific mental health conditions that have arisen most often in my work with transgender youth. In each instance, sorting out these interactions and addressing the mental health problems occurs in the context of supportive counseling for the transgender youth. As mentioned above, both parts may be provided by the same clinician, or more than one clinician may be involved in comprehensive mental health care for a transgender youth. My discussion of these conditions is not meant to provide a method for treating each of these conditions when they arise for transgender youth. This book is designed for experienced mental health clinicians who are already skilled in treating adolescent and young adult mental illness or accessing the necessary specialists or programs to provide treatment. My goal in this chapter is to help you understand how certain common aspects of transgender experience may be incorrectly viewed as mental illness, and how mental illnesses can be exacerbated by gender oppression. My hope is to give you a few thoughts to guide your exploration of transgender identity with youth who also have some of the following mental health concerns:

- anxiety and depression
- self-injury, suicide ideation and substance abuse
- eating disorders
- autism spectrum disorders.

Anxiety and depression
Studies show that:

> [t]rans communities experience higher rates of depression compared to the general population and the non-trans LGB community. Lifetime prevalence of depression in our community may be as high as 50%–67%, compared to 9.1% in the United States overall... This increased risk is related to our experiences of gender discrimination, transphobia, abuse and victimization. (Carmel *et al.* 2014, p.312)

It is also reported that 'the rate of anxiety disorders in trans and gender nonconforming communities is higher than the general population' (Carmel *et al.* 2014, p.316).

Serano describes her cognitive and emotional experience of gender discordance as:

> ...subconsciously seeing myself as female while consciously dealing with the fact that I was male... Sometimes it felt like stress or anxiousness, which led to marathon battles with insomnia. Other times, it surfaced as jealousy or anger at other people who seemed to enjoy taking their gender for granted. But most of all, it felt like sadness to me – a sort of gender sadness – a chronic and persistent grief over the fact that I felt so wrong in my body. (Serano 2007, p.85)

For mild to moderate depression or anxiety that a young person attributes primarily or entirely to experiences related to gender, the approach I have found most helpful and appropriate is to offer validation, affirmation and support for the youth while advocating for fair treatment by family and school. The latter, along with friendships, are the contexts that weigh most heavily in the lives of teens and young adults. Most of the trans youth I worked with got better responses from friends (but not always from the larger peer group) than they did from the adults and institutions in their lives. Some youth will need specific help regarding disclosure, including weighing choices about whom to inform, as well as how and when.

Once these supports are offered, symptoms usually improve. Sometimes they disappear entirely. In these instances, strategies for coping with or reducing symptoms of depression or anxiety may be helpful but are not likely to be the focus of treatment. However, some trans youth attribute their depression or anxiety to other problems or concerns. These will have to be addressed in therapy just as you would for a youth with the same concerns who is not transgender or questioning gender. In all cases, continue to monitor symptoms as the youth gains greater clarity or tries out a social transition. Should symptoms worsen, the treatment approach will need to be reassessed.

For some youth, school problems such as poor concentration, social awkwardness, social anxiety and school refusal turn out to be caused by either the child's inner sense of gender discordance and not fitting in, or by peer rejection or harassment based on gender difference. In these instances the problems improve as gender identity is affirmed and expressed, as long as there is support at school to decrease harassment and increase validation. I have found that some teens who were harassed at school for gender nonconformance saw the harassment diminish or disappear once they presented as a confident young person of their affirmed gender. The peer community respected the trans youth but had lacked compassion for their prior gender nonconforming self.

In cases of severe depression, anxiety, obsessive-compulsive disorder or bipolar disorder, or when the severity of the youth's depression or anxiety causes impairment or danger, treat these concerns first. As with any other severely troubled youth, the clinician must consider safety measures, evaluation for psychiatric medication, and intensive treatment programs as options. Once safety is established, addressing gender concerns will generally help other efforts to lessen distress and impairment.

Self-injury, suicide ideation and substance abuse

Research in Japan shows a self-injury rate of 32 percent in a cohort of trans and gender nonconforming youth. Seventy-four percent had experienced suicide ideation (Hoshiai *et al.* 2010). McManama O'Brien and her colleagues found that among transgender youth:

> ...risk factors for suicide include disclosure of gender identity, family rejection, prior verbal and physical harassment or bullying at school, treatment refusal by a doctor or healthcare provider, and homelessness... In the only known study specifically of MTF and FTM transgender youth, a history of a suicide attempt was significantly associated with experiences of past parental verbal and physical abuse, along with lower body esteem, particularly satisfaction with weight and perceptions of how their bodies were evaluated by others. (McManama O'Brien *et al.* 2016, p.249)

Carmel *et al.* (2014, pp.317–18) point out that substance abuse 'is more common in gender nonconforming communities...and most common in the teens to early twenties' in the general US population. This places trans youth, who are at the intersection of these groups, at great risk. For some, substance use is a way to manage the stress of suppressing a trans identity, the loneliness of not fitting in, the fears of coming out or negative responses from others after coming out. A 2007 survey by Cochran, Peavy and Robohm found that there were very few substance abuse treatment programs specifically designed for LGBT individuals. Trans youth will not feel welcome in recovery programs and rehab facilities that require gender segregation based on assigned sex, nor will they benefit fully from programs that fail to address the impact of stigma, discrimination and microaggression on substance use.

For the most part, disclosures of self-injury, suicide ideation and substance abuse by teens and young adults who were meeting with me regarding gender identity were either not urgent or not current. Current risks need to be addressed with safety steps. Examination of past risks, or current ideation without urge or intent, is an opportunity to uncover the factors contributing to the young person's despair. Most often, for my clients, these have included a sense of hopelessness about being able to live an authentic life with acceptance and free from harassment.

Grossman and D'Augelli conducted focus groups with transgender youth from the New York City metropolitan area. One topic they asked about was risk of self-harm:

> Some consider themselves as having a high risk of self-harm because of their religious backgrounds and the pressures their families and communities put on them to conform to traditional gender behaviors. In the words of one youth (M to F), 'If you come out, you may want to kill yourself if you come from a Catholic background, or Christian, or a very religious background. You love your parents so much you will try to kill yourself to keep them from misery.'
>
> Experiencing rejection and inconsistent caring from most of their parents, schoolmates, teachers, and communities, transgender youth have to constantly fight feelings of shame and unworthiness. As one youth said, 'Throughout my whole life, I was abused physically and mentally by relatives in my family. I have marks on my body. I have things that I remember happened to me.' Some of the youth have distanced themselves from their parents, while others have been forced to leave their homes, which can be an extremely traumatic experience. (Grossman and D'Augelli 2006, pp.124–5)

Ashby Dodge (Dodge, Burke and Oransky 2016) of the Trevor Project, in a presentation at Gender Conference East in 2016, reported that suicide risk for LGBTQ youth is highest just before and after coming out. Some of the factors that increase this risk are gender nonconformance, rejection after coming out and lack of access to support systems. More than one-third of the youth who sought support from the Trevor hotline have lost friends when they came out. Dodge recommends creating a safety plan for coming out, including preparation for negative responses and establishing supports. Beth Burke and Matthew Oransky of Mt. Sinai Hospital, in the same presentation, recommended a range of interventions to address suicidality in gender expansive youth: family therapy, advocacy at school, individual therapy that enhances coping skills, increasing social connections and support and consideration of appropriate medical interventions. They highlighted the importance of helping young people link their suicidal feelings to their experiences of oppression.

Examining the sources of a young trans person's despair leads to a discussion of the authentic self, desires for transition, expectations of what transition will bring and perceived obstacles. Addressing the latter with concrete steps such as family therapy, intervention at school or consideration of medical interventions is most helpful in lessening the sense of hopelessness. Outline future possibilities and realistic time frames if steps cannot be taken right now. For most transgender youth, connections with others through a local support group or some of the resources in Appendix B reduce loneliness and increase the sense of attainable possibilities. Research has shown that protective factors include support by parents, other adults and peers, along with school safety, access to desired medical services and having documents that match one's gender identity (McManama O'Brien *et al.* 2016).

Sometimes a youth's despair is tied directly to a feeling of impatience about medical transition, whether it is the parents or the therapist or both who are requiring more time to agree to this plan. In my experience, the impatience is more often related to temperament than to how long the youth has been waiting. After making an assessment for safety and clinical depression, and referring for medication evaluation, inpatient care or intensive outpatient treatment if needed, I try to ease the youth's impatience. I point out the following: It is fortunate, and not necessarily common, to have parents who are engaged in treatment; this is likely to lead to parental agreement over time; and the long-term outcomes are best for those who have parental support. Hence it will likely be worth the wait. I mention that even the most open-minded and supportive therapist needs some time to complete an evaluation for referral, and parents often change their views in a few weeks or months. I acknowledge that these delays will postpone the resolution of their distress but they are unavoidable and will, in my opinion, lead to the best long-term outcome. I then focus on whatever can be addressed at that time to help ease their distress, including family or school changes, social transition steps and participation in support groups.

Those who are in the early or middle stages of puberty have the greatest sense that time is of the essence, as they are in the midst of physical changes that are entirely wrong for them. In these instances, one must also consider urging the parents to accept earlier intervention with puberty blockers or cross-sex hormones as a possible safety measure, rather than just trying to help the youth be more patient. Tishelman *et al.* write:

> Optimally, a[n]...adolescent should be stable, safe, and supported in advance of receiving medical interventions such as puberty blockers or cross-sex hormones. However, for many, medical intervention is an antidote for some of their mental health problems. This poses a dilemma for the clinician, who may be averse to going forward with medical intervention, but feel compelled to do so in case that is the critical step needed to jump start a child's recovery. Such intervention should only take place once the crisis of active suicidal ideation, behavior and/or self-harm has receded, and after a full psychosocial evaluation if

it had not taken place already, as well as with close monitoring to ensure that the child is safe and that the dangers continue to remit. Delays can be particularly difficult and contribute to a child's distress because of the limited physiological time frame. At the very least, psychological services should help to ensure adequate support systems before any medical intervention occurs, and puberty blockers can buy time and allow for a child to make thoughtful decisions about his or her gender. (Tishelman *et al.* 2015, p.42)

The American Psychological Association Task Force on Gender Identity and Gender Variance reports that research shows much lower rates of suicide among transgender adults after transition (Schneider *et al.* 2009, p.43). While one cannot extrapolate directly from adults to teens, this research does offer hope that facilitating gender transition reduces suicide risk. At the same time, we cannot let our guard down about suicide risk for teens and young adults who have transitioned with family and community support. Sadly, there are reports of youth who had that support yet committed suicide (Abeni 2015). It is good clinical practice to ask all transgender teens about these risk feelings and behaviors at intake and ongoing, especially at times of frustration or disappointed expectations.

Self-harm by transgender youth may or may not be focused on body parts that are most discordant for the youth, such as cutting one's chest. Similarly, substance use may or may not be triggered by feelings of gender dysphoria or despair about access to gender affirmation. Treatment of these problems should include discussion of any gender-related aspects, with compassion for the deep despair some youth feel about their gender struggle. At the same time, provide the treatment you would for a youth with self-injury or substance use who is not transgender or questioning gender. Whether this treatment is folded into the gender supportive counseling or provided by others will depend on the severity of the symptoms and the skill, experience and comfort of the clinician. As with other symptoms discussed above, self-harm and substance abuse may lessen or resolve with gender affirmation. But it is not reasonable to assume they will or to delay direct treatment of these dangerous conditions.

Eating disorders

There may be some confusion about whether a trans youth's distress about their body is related to gender identity or is an eating disorder. Weight gain can appear to a youth of either assigned sex to exacerbate what they see as the gendered shape of their body. Sex hormones cause fat to be distributed differently in pubertal males and females. A transgender youth may try to lose weight to an unhealthy degree with the goal of changing what they view as too masculine or feminine an appearance, rather than because of an irrational sense of overweight. Or they may overeat to hide their feminine or masculine body shape. In cases where this question arises, assessment by a clinician well versed in eating disorders as well as gender identity is best. Otherwise, tandem assessments by two clinicians may be needed.

A young person who is seeking cross-sex hormone therapy should hear from their doctor that they need to be at a healthy weight for safe medical treatment. As they learn more about hormone treatment, they will realize that good nutrition is necessary for some of the benefits of hormonal intervention, particularly fat redistribution and muscle development. This information, along with the knowledge that hormonal intervention is accessible, can be a motivator for healthier eating.

Autism spectrum disorders

There is growing evidence of a higher incidence of autism spectrum disorders (ASD) in transgender populations, when compared to the general population (Shumer *et al.* 2016; Tishelman *et al.* 2015). Research has shown the incidence of ASD in children and adolescents treated at a gender identity clinic to be ten times the rate in the general youth population (de Vries *et al.* 2010). Other researchers found the incidence of gender variance in a group of patients diagnosed with ASD to be seven times the rate in the general population (Janssen, Huang and Duncan 2016). Anecdotal experience, including my own and that of therapists I supervise, suggests that clinicians working with transgender teens and young adults find a significant number of their clients have prior diagnoses of ASD. Some of these diagnoses may simply reflect the social awkwardness that can result from an inner sense of gender discordance and not fitting in with one's assigned gender group. May, Pang and Williams in their 2016 review of the National Database for Autism Research found that:

> The rate of gender variance in the ASD group was higher than that found in non-referred samples of children and adolescents, but the rate was not different than the sample of those clinically referred for mental health problems... Hence, it remains unclear whether the elevated risk of gender variance is specific to ASD or more broadly associated with neurodevelopmental and other psychiatric disorders of childhood. (May *et al.* 2016, p.6)

While the research is not conclusive, all of these studies recommend being cognizant of a potential overlap of ASD and transgender identity.

It is sensible and customary to take longer with the gender identity evaluation of a youth with ASD, to gain adequate clarity about the youth's identity and needs. Annelou de Vries and her colleagues in Amsterdam found the following:

> For clinical management, our findings on clinical characteristics of individuals with co-occurring gender dysphoria and ASD have consequences. In all cases described, the diagnostic procedure was extended to disentangle whether the gender dysphoria evolved from a general feeling of being 'different' or a 'core' cross-gender identity. Most helpful seemed an individual approach that took into consideration that rigid and concrete thinking around gender roles and difficulty developing aspects of personal identity may play a part. (de Vries *et al.* 2010, p.36)

Here are some questions that arise when evaluating a transgender youth who also has ASD, followed by my answers (please keep in mind that what I offer here is based on my experiences with a small number of transgender clients with ASD and the few articles written so far on this subject):

1. How do we determine that the transgender identity is not just an intense interest typical of ASD and likely to pass?
2. How might the evaluation proceed differently with a trans person with ASD?
3. How does the social transition differ for a person with ASD?

1. HOW DO WE DETERMINE THAT THE YOUTH'S EXPRESSION OF TRANSGENDER IDENTITY IS NOT JUST AN INTENSE INTEREST TYPICAL OF ASD AND LIKELY TO PASS?

This is often the first question raised by parents or clinicians about a person with ASD who expresses a transgender identity. One of the *DSM-5* criteria for ASD is abnormally intense or restricted interests (American Psychiatric Association 2013). Tony Attwood (2015) notes that these interests tend to be either collections of unusual objects (i.e., not those other children typically collect) or the acquisition of overly detailed information on a particular subject. This suggests that these interests are about something external to the individual rather than a claim of a different identity.

In my experience, it has been easy to engage clients with ASD in lengthy discussion about these fixated interests, while they had little detail to offer about their sense of gender identity. They just insisted this is who they are. Think for a moment of how you would explain your own sense of certainty about your gender identity if you were not allowed to mention your body characteristics and the assumptions others had about your gender as proof. Most of us could not say more than 'I just know I am female/male. I never really gave it much thought.' This is the experience of many youth who are asked to explain how they know their gender, and young people with ASD are even less equipped to manufacture conversation about it. They may be insistent and persistent in expressing their affirmed gender and related needs. But they may not be able to go into the lengthy discourse typical of their 'discussion' of a fixation that is an indicator of ASD.

2. HOW MIGHT THE EVALUATION PROCEED DIFFERENTLY WITH A TRANS PERSON WITH ASD?

The ASD diagnosis covers youth with a wide range of functioning. Severe autism includes the individual with extremely limited speech who does not seek interaction with others (American Psychiatric Association 2013). These individuals are unlikely to express a transgender identity or request gender affirmation or transition. Youth with ASD or with symptoms that may suggest ASD who are requesting help with gender identity are likely to be functioning in the mild to moderate range of ASD. Symptoms can include deficits in social communication, difficulty initiating social interactions and decreased interest in social interaction, along with the fixated interests mentioned above.

With this in mind, let's take a look at the four foci of gender identity evaluation outlined in Chapter 6: sense of self, group affiliation, body and regard. In my experience, sense of self and body discomfort have been the prominent concerns for trans individuals with ASD. The other two factors, group affiliation and how others regard us, are highly social factors. The less an individual is socially focused, the less these factors will be present in their experience of gender discordance. With limited social focus there may be less motivation or ability to experience social transition as a step in learning more about oneself. There will also be less discussion in therapy about social factors in gender transition.

Some individuals with ASD will not express a detailed narrative about their gender. The evaluation necessitates patience, asking numerous questions in different ways at different times to see if a consistent picture of Gender Dysphoria emerges. It can be difficult to fill the standard 50-minute session with discussion. Briefer sessions with less frequency may be more helpful than weekly full-length sessions. The need for a slow, repetitious and question-heavy discourse is not limited to people with ASD. It is also helpful with those young people who are less talkative or have had less opportunity to reflect on their feelings with friends to create a coherent narrative of their experiences.

3. HOW DOES THE SOCIAL TRANSITION DIFFER FOR A PERSON WITH ASD?

Individuals with ASD may be less interested in, or less capable of, a social transition. Being socially awkward, they may dread calling attention to themselves as one necessarily does when making a social transition. If they are socially isolated, they are unlikely to have a peer group who will embrace them in their affirmed gender and in what to others appears to be a cross-gender presentation. Those in special schools or classes may have the benefit of staff who will guide peers to respond in an accepting and validating manner.

Theory of Mind (ToM) refers to 'the ability to recognize and understand thoughts, beliefs, desires and intentions of other people in order to make sense of their behaviour and predict what they are going to do next' (Attwood 2015, p.124). Impaired ToM in people with ASD may lead to a limited ability to grasp how others view their gender identity. A transgender individual with these deficits may not realize the value of offering cues to others through grooming, clothes and manner, to help others see them in their affirmed gender. It may not be enough to simply inform peers of a new name and pronouns, for example, and expect the social transition to be fully understood and validated even by well-meaning others.

In their discussion of a youth with ASD who experienced difficulties with the interpersonal aspects of her gender transition, Laura Jacobs and her colleagues state:

> [once she] understood her identity to be female, she assumed her peers would automatically adopt the same understanding... Though 'internally transitioned' nothing had altered in her appearance or demeanor, and she expressed surprise that no

one noticed the change. It became clear that she suffered an impaired ToM: She was unable to appreciate that others might see her differently than she saw herself, or that others would have a need to gradually come to terms with [her] new identity. (Jacobs *et al.* 2014, p.280)

The authors suggest coaching clients with deficits in ToM about the need to take steps to help others understand who they are.

Our understanding of how to help trans youth with ASD is still evolving. Reaching certainty about gender identity as well as whether, when and how to carry out transition steps can be expected to take longer for teens and young adults with social deficits.

FOR FURTHER EXPLORATION

Books and articles

'Gender dysphoria and co-occurring autism spectrum disorders: Review, case examples, and treatment considerations,' by Laura Jacobs, Katherine Rachlin, Laura Erickson-Schroth and Aron Janssen, *LGBT Health 1*, 4, 277–82, 2014.

'Mental Health Concerns,' by Tamar Carmel, Ruben Hopwood and lore m. dickey, in *Trans Bodies, Trans Selves* (edited by Laura Erickson-Schroth), Oxford University Press, 2014.

'Transgender youth: Invisible and vulnerable,' by Arnold Grossman and Anthony D'Augelli, *Journal of Homosexuality 51*, 1, 111–28, 2006.

TRANSITION

CHAPTER 8

Social Transition

The social transition consists of any or all of the following, accompanied by a declaration to others of one's affirmed gender identity:

- adopting a new name and/or new pronouns
- different clothing, hairstyling, jewelry, makeup
- for masculine transition, binding and packing
- for feminine transition: tucking, voice training and hair removal
- changing name and gender marker on documents.

NAME, PRONOUNS, CLOTHES AND GROOMING

The individual making the social transition informs some or all of their family, friends, school peers, co-workers and so on that they now affirm a gender that is different from the sex they were assigned at birth. As part of this disclosure they let others know of any new name or pronoun set they would like others to use in referring to them. This is a simple request that may elicit complex responses. When the youth is comfortable telling everyone in their life, and others respond respectfully, this part of the process goes smoothly. When the individual is only comfortable disclosing this information in some contexts, or when others do not respond with respect, the social transition is more challenging. Allies who speak up to those who disrespect the youth's wishes are a great help. The social transition can be full-time or part-time. In the latter case it is generally limited to contexts in which the individual feels safe to try out their affirmed gender expression. This safety may be related to risks of rejection, harassment, violence or loss of housing, employment and so on.

I generally recommend that the youth defer to their parents when it comes to informing people whose response matters more to the parents than to the young person. This is likely to include parents' co-workers, adult friends who don't interact often with the youth and some extended family members. This suggestion should not be taken to mean that it is OK to put the youth in situations where they have to change their presentation to hide who they are from these adults; just that if they are not seeing any of these adults in the near future, it is fine for parents to take their time before informing everyone. Extended family members should certainly be informed before a family gathering that includes the youth. Otherwise the youth will have to revert from social transition to self-denial for the occasion.

Prior to the social transition, I recommend that parents inform only their closest friends and family members of the young person's gender exploration, as needed for the youth's or the parents' support. Once a social transition is imminent, other adults can be told in person, by phone, by letter or in an email. It is important to present this new information in a positive, affirming manner. The goal is to tell others that the youth has realized something essential about their gender identity, and to request a respectful response from everyone. Often parents mention how happy their child is since affirming their gender identity.

As part of the social transition, most teens and young adults make changes in their appearance, in part as a way to signal to others how they want to be viewed. This can include changing hair length, hairstyle, clothing, use of jewelry or makeup and any other signifiers of gender or gender ambiguity. These changes help others understand and remember the youth's affirmed gender, while also allowing the youth to feel more congruence between inner and outer self. For those who were previously prohibited from expressing this aspect of themselves, or who were scorned for doing so, the social transition can bring a strong sense of self-affirmation.

Trans people vary in the extent to which they care about *passing*, which is the process of presenting oneself to be seen consistently as one's affirmed gender (Ettner 1996, p.116; Keo-Meier and Hicks 2014). Most cisgender people make some effort to pass. At some point in our life we have made choices regarding these same facets of presentation (hairstyle, clothing, jewelry or makeup) to present ourselves to others in a way that better conforms to societal ideas of femininity or masculinity. Some cisgender people have used exercise or surgery to modify their bodies to appear more masculine or feminine to fit in better with visual expectations for their assigned sex. We are constantly bombarded with images and comments that inform us what these expectations are. Some trans people also make an effort to pass and do not want to be read or *clocked* by others as trans. Some trans people are unconcerned about this. While the social transition always involves informing someone about one's affirmed gender identity, steps related to presentation are taken by some trans people and not by others. The focus of each step taken may be on passing more easily, or on feeling more comfortable inside, or neither or both of these concerns may predominate. Each trans person is unique and each social transition is as well.

Living *stealth* is the decision to live in one's affirmed gender without letting others know that one has transitioned to that gender. Obviously, this can only be done among those who did not know the person when they were living in their birth-assigned gender. Some trans people prefer the word 'private,' feeling that 'stealth' has a connotation of 'sneaking around, or getting away with doing something wrong' (Reynolds and Goldstein 2014, p.136).

From a therapist's point of view, the value of the social transition derives from the youth having the opportunity to experience living in their affirmed gender and being regarded by others in the affirmed gender. If others' responses are supportive, the social transition usually leads to some alleviation of distress or reduction in the frequency, severity or presence of psychological symptoms caused or exacerbated by gender dysphoria. Whether or not the youth was previously in significant distress, the social transition usually leads to happiness from living more authentically. The social transition also provides information for the young person and their parents about the youth's gender identity. The youth has an opportunity to try out one or more gender presentations, other than the one assigned at birth, and determine which gender presentation feels congruent with their inner identity. They also get a sense of the varied ways others will respond and how they feel in reaction to these responses. This will help them understand what they may be facing as they transition, and enable them to plan accordingly. If the environment turns out to be hostile, the family has an opportunity to pause and make changes to improve the environment or change their circumstances to allow for a safe and supportive transition.

Social transition for non-binary youth is different in one important way from a transition between binary gender categories. Since we do not have any cultural conventions to signal a non-binary gender identity, these identities generally have to be disclosed verbally whenever the individual wants to be understood authentically. Androgynous presentations may be read as non-binary in 'queer' circles, but are likely to be confusing to most other observers. While a trans person can make efforts to pass as female or male, and elicit affirming responses from respectful strangers, people of non-binary gender identity do not have that option. Most have to handle varied responses, assumptions and uncertainties from others.

BINDING, PACKING AND TUCKING

Teens and young adults who have experienced breast development in puberty are aware that breasts are one of the visual cues others use to determine female gender. For trans youth who identify as male or non-binary, breast development is often distressing. Breasts are incongruent with the individual's gender. A *binder* is a garment used to flatten the chest. It helps the individual be less aware of their breasts and present with a more masculine body profile. Binders can be ordered online. Wearing a binder may bring emotional comfort at the expense of physical discomfort. 'The long-term effects of binding can include breathing problems and back pain' (Teich 2012, p.51). Nick Krieger describes his experience when he began wearing a binder:

> I wrestled it on in the morning before going to work and felt it dig into my skin as I slouched at my desk during the day... The binder, rubbed, scratched and compressed like a panty-hose tank top; breathing on top of an Andean peak would have been easier... But every time I caught my reflection in the mirror, I thought to myself, Goddamn, you look good. So, I kept at it, bearing in mind the blisters, twisted ankles, and foot cramps that every woman with stiletto heels or knee-high boots endured for the sake of appearance. (Krieger 2011, p.34)

Prior to getting a binder, many transmasculine youths will wear multiple layers of clothing and stoop to hide their breasts. Arin Andrews describes it this way: 'I realized that if I hunched over, I could make them disappear somewhat into my shirt. I started to walk with my shoulders forward' (2014, p.41). Body structures vary widely. Not all individuals who would like to create the feel and appearance of a male chest can do so effectively and with reasonable comfort using a binder. For them, the need for top surgery is likely to feel more urgent.

Gaffs and packers are used to create the visual appearance as well as the physical sense of having genitals that conform to one's affirmed gender. A *gaff* is a garment used to tuck the penis under to create the feel and appearance of more feminine genitals. A *packer* is something placed in the underwear to create the feel and appearance of male genitalia. Gaffs and packers can be homemade or purchased on the internet. As with so many of the choices contemplated by transgender youth, use of a gaff or a packer is a very personal decision. Many cis people also use garments to hide or enhance the visual presentation of gendered body parts such as breasts and genitals.

VOICE TRAINING

There is great variation in the degree to which transgender individuals are distressed about any discordance between the sound of their voice and their affirmed gender identity, as well as the extent to which they take steps to address this. Feelings about voice can change over the course of a person's gender transition. Congruence of speech and gender identity may be important to an individual, whether they are transitioning from male to female, female to male or from either assigned sex to a non-binary gender identity. Those who transition with testosterone can expect the pitch of their voice to become lower in the course of hormone therapy. Those who transition with estrogen, however, do not experience any change in pitch from hormone treatment (Davies and Goldberg 2006; Davies, Papp and Antoni 2015).

Shelagh Davies and Joshua Goldberg found that 'changes to the gendered aspects of communication can help reduce gender dysphoria and facilitate gender presentation that is consistent with the felt sense of self, resulting in improved mental health and quality of life' (2006, p.167). Pitch is the primary factor in others' perception of a speaker's gender. Intonation patterns, the melody in spoken sentences, also differ between cisgender speakers of different genders, but fundamental frequency, the habitual pitch while speaking, is a stronger indicator than intonation (King, Brown and McCrea 2011).

There is a large overlap in the pitch frequencies of cisgender male and female voices. Speaking fundamental frequencies in the range of 145–175 Hz are considered gender neutral (Davies *et al.* 2015). An individual whose average pitch is below this range can learn to elevate their voice if they do not want to be read by others as male. Attention to intonation can enhance the femininity of the voice. Among English speakers, cisgender females tend to have rising tones while the speech of cisgender males is flatter (Davies *et al.* 2015; King *et al.* 2011). Individuals transitioning to male may practice stereotypically male intonation patterns as their vocal pitch drops from testosterone. Intonation patterns are specific to language and culture and may be practiced as well by cisgender individuals who feel pressure to conform to gender-based expectations.

Those who wish to adjust their speech to fit the typical pitch and patterns associated with their affirmed gender can practice on their own, with or without the aid of available videos or apps, or they can seek the guidance of a speech therapist who specializes in transgender voice. Working with a speech therapist protects against damaging the voice in one's efforts to alter pitch (Davies *et al.* 2015). Many transgender individuals are comfortable with their voice as it is, or unconcerned about whether their voice signals to others that they are transgender. They recognize that there are cisgender men with higher voices and cis women with lower voices. Some of these cisgender people also experience misgendering on the basis of their voice, especially in phone calls where voice is the only gender cue. Presumably they, too, have a range of responses to this circumstance, which may or may not include efforts to alter the gendered aspects of their voice.

HAIR REMOVAL

Facial hair is a strong visual indicator of male identity, as is an abundance of body hair. These features do not change significantly in treatment with female hormones. Many people transitioning to female or non-binary identities after male puberty take steps to alter the masculine appearance of facial hair, and sometimes of body hair, by shaving closely, covering with makeup, or undergoing electrolysis or laser treatments. Permanent hair removal is expensive, time-consuming and sometimes painful. These services are not covered by health insurance as they are viewed as cosmetic rather than as essential to alleviation of gender discordance. One might compare this to chest surgery for cisgender males with breast tissue they find gender discordant. That condition is labeled 'Gynecomastia' and the surgery is covered by insurance. It is not dismissed as a cosmetic issue.

Those who are seeking professional help for hair removal should inquire in advance if the practitioner welcomes transgender clients. A recommendation from others in the trans community is helpful.

DOCUMENTATION

The most important point about legal documentation is that the ID a person carries should match how they are presenting in public. This increases the likelihood that they will be affirmed in their gender identity by others and reduces the likelihood of harassment (Wu and Broadus 2012). Therefore, documentation changes should be underway once someone has affirmed their gender identity and, if possible, has tried out a social transition to confirm their intentions to live in the affirmed gender. This is true for adolescents as well as young adults. Documentation is an important safety concern. Parents who fear a youth will have a change of heart even after a confirming social transition can be reassured that in that unlikely event the documentation changes can be reversed.

Regulations regarding changes to legal name and gender marker vary widely. An individual's ability to make these changes may depend on whether they can afford to pay fees and obtain medical care. Medical transition with hormones or surgery is a prerequisite for some document changes in some localities. In the United States, legal name change requires submitting an application, paying a fee, parental agreement if one is under age 18 and then a hearing before a judge. If one or more legal parents object to the name change, a youth under 18 will most likely need representation by an attorney (Paakkonen 2012). A few weeks after the name change is approved in probate court, a document verifying the name change arrives in the mail. The name change should be approved unless a person is using it to evade criminal charges or unpaid debts (Wu and Broadus 2012). The document provided is the proof needed to change one's name on other legal and financial documents. Thus, name change in the United States happens through a single legal procedure although informing relevant institutions and registries of the name change is a multi-step process.

Gender marker change in the United States does not happen via a single transaction. There are separate procedures and requirements for changing one's gender marker for Social Security, passport, birth certificate and driver license or state ID. For this reason, there is not a single moment when a person has legally changed their gender. For financial and other reasons, not everyone has access to every legal gender marker change they desire at the point in time they wish to make the change. Rules vary from state to state for birth certificate and license changes. In the United States there is no gender marker for people who are non-binary, while Australia now has a designation of 'X' on passports for people who are neither female nor male (Transgender Australia 2015). See Appendix B for a list of transgender advocacy organizations worldwide that can help answer questions about documentation changes.

FOR FURTHER EXPLORATION

Books and articles

'Social Transition,' by Heath Mackenzie Reynolds and Zil Garner Goldstein, in *Trans Bodies, Trans Selves* (edited by Laura Erickson-Schroth), Oxford University Press, 2014.

Transgender Family Law: A Guide to Effective Practice, edited by Jennifer Levi and Elizabeth Monnin-Browder, Author House, 2012.

The Voice Book for Trans and Non-Binary People: A Practical Guide to Creating and Sustaining Authentic Voice and Communication, by Matthew Mills and Gillie Stoneham, Jessica Kingsley Publishers, 2017.

CHAPTER 9

Medical Transition

Medical interventions to assist with gender transition for youth can include one or more of the following:

- puberty blockers
- cross-sex hormones
- top surgery
- breast augmentation, facial feminization and trachea shave
- hysterectomy and orchiectomy
- genital reconstruction surgery (GRS).

All of the surgeries on this list are considered *gender affirmation surgeries*. Hysterectomy, orchiectomy and genital reconstruction surgeries are sometimes referred to collectively as *bottom surgeries*. You may also see GRS referred to as SRS: sex reassignment surgery. Currently GRS is the preferred term. Top surgery is the most common surgery sought by transgender youth.

PUBERTY BLOCKERS

Puberty blockers are medical treatments that delay the onset of puberty or halt the progress of puberty. They allow a young person more time to gain clarity about their gender identity without going through pubertal developments that may in the long run be wrong for them. For natal females, puberty blockers will prevent menstruation and breast development, and allow continued growth in height. For natal males, puberty blockers will prevent enlargement of the voice box (which causes a deeper voice and a visible Adam's apple), facial hair and increased body hair, and masculinization of the facial structure.

Puberty blockers are most effective when they are started immediately after the onset of puberty. Current practice dictates that the young person should experience some pubertal changes before receiving puberty blockers to clarify that they are not just distressed about the idea of puberty but also experience distress about its actual onset (Hembree *et al.* 2009). Olson, Forbes and Belzer note: 'The beginning signs of puberty in transgender children often bring increased body dysphoria and the potential development of a whole host of comorbidities including depression, anxiety, illicit substance use, high-risk sexual behaviors, and increased suicidality' (2011, p.174). It is important to anticipate the option of puberty blockers when counseling pre-pubertal trans and gender nonconforming children, and discuss this option in advance.

There are no transgender medical interventions prior to the onset of puberty. Children who express a gender identity that is not in keeping with their assigned sex can be monitored by their pediatrician so the onset of puberty is detected and puberty blockers can be offered at the most opportune time. For those who begin puberty blocker treatment and later decide that they are in fact comfortable with the pubertal development of their natal sex, puberty blockers are discontinued and their body proceeds with its innate pubertal development, just delayed by the time on blockers (Canadian Pediatric Endocrine Group 2012; Hembree *et al.* 2009; Tishelman *et al.* 2015). Most youth who undergo puberty blocker treatment then go on to begin cross-sex hormone therapy (Olson, Forbes and Belzer 2011). Having avoided the changes of their natal puberty, they are free of the need for certain other interventions, such as top surgery, facial hair removal and facial feminization surgery, that they may have had to undergo had they completed their puberty without medical interruption (Tishelman *et al.* 2015).

To me, the greatest challenge in counseling transgender teens and their parents about puberty blockers and cross-sex hormones is the impact on fertility. Among youth treated at the onset of puberty with puberty blockers, those who later choose to stop blockers and continue with their original puberty will become fertile. However, those who move directly from blockers to cross-sex hormones will not (Olson *et al.* 2011). It is impossible for a teen or a 10-year-old to determine with any certainty how they will feel about becoming a biological parent in adulthood; yet those who begin puberty blockers, and their parents, are agreeing to a treatment plan that will most likely rule out this possibility as most youth do continue from blockers directly to cross-sex hormones. Generally, when asked about this, transgender teens will reply that if they choose to become parents in the future, they will be happy to adopt.

There are only two choices available at this juncture, to remain infertile or to experience unwanted pubertal development. The latter generally outweighs the former in the young person's consideration. Parents and clinicians who are aware of the discordance the youth feels, and understand the unwanted changes of puberty that either cannot be reversed or require surgery to do so, must weigh these matters carefully and decide what they feel is best for this child. For teens who are already well into puberty and contemplating cross-sex hormone therapy, the impact on fertility is different. This is discussed further in the next section in this chapter.

Parents and clinicians grappling with whether to support a child's request for puberty blockers can take some encouragement from a 2014 study by de Vries *et al.* They followed 55 transgender young adults who had received puberty blockers during adolescence and subsequently cross-sex hormone therapy and gender affirmation surgery. Their results showed that these treatments alleviated dysphoria and the individuals in their study had improved psychological functioning. None regretted having undergone treatment. A single case study of a youth (referred to as 'B') who was followed for 22 years after beginning puberty suppression found that there were no unfavorable medical outcomes:

> Pubertal suppression, however, averts the despair of gender dysphoric adolescents because of their physical changes and it may contribute to more self-confidence when socially interacting in adolescence and adulthood. On a day-to-day basis, B did not have to explain himself or defend his choices. He was not harassed or stigmatized. The case of B gives hope that negative side effects of puberty suppression are limited, although the results will have to be confirmed in further studies. (Cohen-Kettenis *et al.* 2011, p.846)

CROSS-SEX HORMONES

For teens and young adults who are past the early stages of puberty, or for teens who have been on puberty blockers, treatment with estrogen or testosterone is used to help the individual's body feminize or masculinize for greater concordance with their gender identity. The effects of these hormone treatments include both irreversible and reversible changes. The primary changes from cross-sex hormone therapy are as follows (Hembree *et al.* 2009; Teich, 2012):

- For those undergoing *feminizing* hormone treatment:
  › softer skin
  › reduced muscle mass
  › increased fat distribution to the hips and buttocks
  › slower loss of scalp hair
  › thinning or lightening of body hair
  › decrease in spontaneous erections, loss of libido
  › breast development.
- For those undergoing *masculinizing* hormone treatment:
  › cessation of menstruation
  › increased muscle mass

> fat redistribution away from hips and buttocks to waist
> deeper voice
> increased facial and body hair, possible male pattern baldness
> clitoral enlargement, increased libido
> possible acne or oily skin.

In addition to the physical changes, some people experience emotional effects of cross-sex hormone therapy. Many report a sense of calm or 'feeling right' shortly after beginning hormone treatment. It is as if the shift in body chemistry helps their mind feel at ease. Other changes are specific to the direction of transition. Feminizing hormones cause some people to express emotion more easily (Teich 2012). Many individuals told me that after starting estrogen they cried more often at touching moments in movies. They generally viewed this in a positive light, as a freeing-up of the emotional constraint caused by their original male physiology. Conversely, 'some transmen may feel that expressing emotions (crying, for instance) is more difficult than it was prior to beginning testosterone' (Teich 2012, p.52). Those transitioning with testosterone often reported increased energy and sometimes a greater likelihood of having aggressive thoughts, such as the idea of striking out at someone who angers them. No one who spoke to me about this reported an increase in aggressive behavior, just in the nature of their inner response.

These changes occur gradually, over the course of months and years. We can view the first few weeks and months of cross-sex hormone treatment as a time of further confirmation of the youth's gender identity. If the first small changes from treatment, or the idea of actually being on hormones, feel discordant to the youth, the treatment can be stopped. For the teens and young adults I have counseled, the early changes from cross-sex hormones have been confirming and exciting. None of my clients has opted to discontinue hormone therapy for this reason. Serano describes the experience:

> Transsexuals will often say that they can never know for sure whether they should physically transition until they begin taking hormones – if they find that they like the changes in their body and the way they feel, then it was the right decision; if not, then it was the wrong one... I honestly was not 100 percent sure that transitioning would ease my gender dissonance until after my first few weeks of being on female hormones. The way they made me feel, and the subsequent changes they brought about in my body, just felt *right*. There is no other way to describe it. (Serano 2007, p.86, italics in original)

This need to try out and see what hormone treatment brings may be even more significant for non-binary individuals. Some of the non-binary youth I have worked with requested low-dose or short-term hormone therapy, either to induce slower and smaller changes or to experience one of the early irreversible changes (a deeper voice) and then discontinue hormones. Many individuals who were assigned female at birth but identify as not-female come to feel that their voice interferes with their ability to be seen as not-female. Some welcome the idea of gaining a deeper voice without having to remain on testosterone long term. My few clients who approached hormone therapy this way ended up continuing the treatment longer term, feeling more fully confirmed by their initial experiences on hormones. How this question will be addressed by other non-binary individuals, both transmasculine and transfeminine, remains to be seen.

Jennifer Hastings has these recommendations for non-binary hormone therapy:

> The approach to hormone therapy should be guided by the person's desired configuration of secondary sex characteristics. Strategies may include using hormones at a lower dose or for a limited period of time. Nonbinary people on the feminine spectrum may choose to only use an androgen blocker, and/or use estrogen at a very low dose, or for a short time. For those on

the masculine spectrum, low dose testosterone can be acceptable, especially if menses is not a source of dysphoria, as low dose may not stop menses. If gender dysphoria worsens with menses, testosterone may be increased... Some desired combinations of results (such as a deepened voice without facial or body hair growth) may not be possible. (Hastings 2016)

Endocrine Society guidelines and the practices of many medical centers specialized in treating transgender youth recommend 16 years of age as a threshold for eligibility for cross-sex hormone therapy (de Vries, Cohen-Kettenis and Delemarre-van de Waal 2006; Hembree *et al.* 2009; Tishelman *et al.* 2015). In my experience, making this decision on a case-by-case basis brings greater clarity to the question of what is best for a given youth, rather than working with strict age-based guidelines. Currently, among those who treat substantial numbers of transgender youth there are 'differing assumptions regarding...whether cross-sex hormones and surgery should be offered to youth, and if so, at what age' (Tishelman *et al.* 2015, p.42). I will discuss this further in Chapter 10.

For a youth who has already developed reproductive capacity, cross-sex hormones have an unknown impact on future fertility (Hembree *et al.* 2009). The youth and the family can consider sperm banking or egg harvesting for the best chances of being able to have a biologically related child in the future. However, the collection and storage fees for sperm banking are more expensive than some families can afford. Egg harvesting is more complicated and intrusive. It is also more expensive and has less certain future viability. Most of my transgender teen clients (as well as most of the transgender adults that I have counseled) have stated that if they choose to become parents in the future they will be happy to adopt. Their options at this juncture are similar to those for youth considering puberty blockers: to risk infertility or to remain with a physiology that is incongruent with their gender. Gender congruence generally outweighs fertility in the young person's consideration. Parents and clinicians must weigh these matters carefully when the youth is under 18 and needs their approval to access hormone therapy.

TOP SURGERY

In my years of counseling transgender youth and their parents, top surgery was the surgery most often sought by youth and most easily endorsed by their parents. 'Top surgery' is shorthand for breast removal with male chest reconstruction. Top surgery affords numerous benefits that do not come with wearing a binder: the ability to be shirtless in the summer, to move and breathe freely, to dress lightly in warm weather, to have a masculine body profile even if one originally had large breasts, and to stand tall without feeling the need to stoop to hide one's chest. I have been touched by the sense of freedom and pride shown by many trans youths the first time I saw them after chest surgery. Some seemed to have grown a few inches in the process of standing tall. Non-binary youth as well as those transitioning to male may seek top surgery as part of their medical transition.

Most often, transgender youth pursue top surgery 6–12 months after starting testosterone. This gives them time to experience the gradual masculinization of hormone therapy, both in how they feel about themselves and in the impact it has on their interactions with others. Once they feel further confirmed in their masculine identity, they may feel increased urgency about having top surgery. Having breasts alongside more masculine features can heighten body dysphoria. For this reason, I think it is best to alert parents that the decision to initiate hormone therapy is a step toward the likely emotional need for top surgery within a year.

Testosterone treatment generally precedes top surgery for trans male youths because its effects are gradual, leaving open the possibility of them changing their mind. It also does not expose the youth to the risks that come with surgery. These factors make it more acceptable to parents who may still have some doubts about their child's gender identity. There may, however, be instances when top surgery makes sense as a first step. I have found this to be the case with a number of adults that I have counseled who identify as male. With the increase in individuals identifying as transmasculine or other not-female non-binary identities, requests for top surgery without the intention of hormonal transition are likely to increase. Gender non-binary people may, in fact, 'pursue a variety of gender affirming surgeries and procedures, including chest reconstruction or breast augmentation and genital surgeries' (Hastings 2016).

Those planning for top surgery should build in adequate time for recovery if they wish for their surgical scars to remain as thin as possible. Some youths are anxious to resume exercise to maintain or build a more masculine physique. They will be advised by their surgeon to refrain from upper body exercise for a number of weeks after surgery (Chyten-Brennan 2014).

BREAST AUGMENTATION, FACIAL FEMINIZATION AND TRACHEA SHAVE

These three procedures differ from the others discussed in this chapter in that they are generally not covered by health insurance, even by those plans that reimburse for other trans-related health care. They are viewed as cosmetic, despite being essential to the well-being of many transgender individuals. In my experience, these surgeries are more likely to be sought by adult trans women than by trans youth. Some trans people, medical practitioners and legal rights organizations have begun to advocate for health insurance coverage for these services. Access to these interventions is sharply curtailed by the financial limitations of many of the women who need them.

Breast augmentation is sought when breast development from feminizing hormones is not satisfactory. As stated in Coleman *et al.* (2011, p.59): 'Although not an explicit criterion, it is recommended that MtF patients undergo feminizing hormone therapy (minimum 12 months) prior to breast augmentation surgery. The purpose is to maximize breast growth in order to obtain better surgical (aesthetic) results.'

Some women seek facial feminization surgery to feminize the masculine aspects of their facial features that developed in male puberty. The surgeon makes adjustments to the facial bone structure, creating a more feminine visage. Changes may be made to the brow, the nose, the cheeks, the jaw or the chin (Teich 2012).

A tracheal shave, to reduce the prominence of the Adam's apple, may be done at the same time or separately.

HYSTERECTOMY AND ORCHIECTOMY

Hysterectomy (removal of the uterus) and related surgeries (removal of the ovaries, fallopian tubes or cervix) may be desired by those undergoing masculine transition, because these organs are incongruent with their gender, to reduce their production of sex hormones, to be free of annual gynecology visits or out of concern about the effects of testosterone treatment on the reproductive organs. Teich (2012, p.55) states: 'There is debate among medical professionals about the long-term effects of testosterone on the FTM reproductive system, and some doctors recommend a hysterectomy and/or oophorectomy [removal of ovaries] as a prophylactic measure.'

Orchiectomy (removal of the testicles) is included in MTF genital reconstruction surgery (GRS, see below), but it can also be performed as a stand-alone procedure to reduce the body's production of testosterone (Deutsch 2014). Orchiectomy by itself may be sought by trans women who cannot afford GRS or who have not decided to go ahead with GRS.

These surgeries, along with GRS, have an obvious impact on fertility. Youth who elect these surgeries, and their parents if they are under 18, can investigate preservation of fertility via sperm banking or egg harvesting. To date, these surgeries are only rarely offered to those under age 18. Informed consent for these surgeries, as for hormone therapy, requires disclosure and discussion of the expected impact on fertility.

GENITAL RECONSTRUCTION SURGERY (GRS)

Genital surgeries are less often accessed by transgender youth because of the expense, the need to have lived fully in the affirmed gender for a year prior to referral for surgery, and the long waiting lists of the more experienced surgeons. In the United States these surgeries have generally been offered only for those over age 18, although some surgeons and hospitals have accepted youths referred at age 17. Many trans youth feel less urgency for genital surgery as their genitals are not part of their public presentation. According to Chyten-Brennan (2014, p.276), 'Top surgery is more common than bottom surgery for those of us on the transmasculine spectrum because it costs less and has a greater impact on our outward appearance.' Many transgender individuals are comfortable with their genitalia and for that reason do not seek genital surgery. Others decline the surgeries because of the risks involved, some uncertainties in outcomes and the likelihood that surgical safety and outcomes will improve over time.

Those who pursue genital surgery may have a variety of reasons for doing so, as Cotten explains:

[Many trans men] feel driven or compelled to change and align our genitals with our gender to feel fully integrated and whole. Genital surgery can also open doors to social bonding and intimacy with others that are inaccessible or feel too risky to pursue without genitals that match our gender presentations... Many trans men [who] feel uncomfortable and/or unsafe disrobing in locker rooms and public showers...may come to feel that they are missing out on valuable experiences and relationships with others. Genitoplasty [genital surgery] also opens up opportunities for romantic and sexual intimacy. It is difficult for some men to face their genitals in the mirror in private, and the prospect of explaining them to a potential lover or someone to whom we are attracted can feel daunting, scary and even shameful. (Cotten 2012, p.1)

Janet Mock (2014, p.227) describes her interest in GRS this way: 'I sought something greater than the changing of genitalia. I was seeking reconciliation with myself.' She goes on to say:

> I didn't dwell on the risks because there was no other alternative for me. This surgery...was the step I'd known I had to take ever since I was old enough to know it was a possibility... The procedure made me no longer feel as self-conscious about my body, which made me more confident and helped me to be more completely myself. (Mock 2014, p.230)

Individuals considering GRS are advised to do extensive research on these surgeries, the outcomes and risks and the surgeons who provide them before making any decisions. They need to be aware of and prepared for the recovery period and the aftercare. The Gender Identity Research and Education Society (GIRES) lists the following options for surgical intervention for *trans men*:

- hysterectomy (removal of the uterus)
- salpingo-oophorectomy (removal of the fallopian tubes and ovaries)
- vaginectomy (removal of the vagina)
- metoidioplasty (creates a micro-penis by bringing the clitoris forward)
- urethroplasty (creates a repositioned, longer urethra, joined to the existing urethra)
- scrotoplasty (creates a scrotum and generally includes testicular prostheses, often at a later stage)
- phalloplasty (creates a penis)
- erectile implants (creates erectile capability).

(adapted from Curtis et al. 2015, p.7)

GIRES lists these options for surgical intervention for *trans women*:

- penectomy (removal of the penis)
- orchidectomy or orchiectomy (removal of the testicles)

- vaginoplasty (creation of a vagina)
- clitoroplasty (creation of a clitoris)
- labioplasty (creation of labia)
- repositioning of the urethra.

(adapted from GIRES 2016, p.11)

Some of the factors affecting decisions about genital surgeries are cost, insurance coverage, possible effects on sexual pleasure and relationships, effects on fertility, lack of safety when genitalia do not match gender presentation, cosmetic outcomes, urinary outcomes and general surgical risks (Chyten-Brennan 2014).

FOR FURTHER EXPLORATION

Books and articles

'Endocrine treatment of transsexual persons: An Endocrine Society clinical practice guideline,' by Hembree *et al.*, *Journal of Clinical Endocrinology and Metabolism 94*, 9, 3132–54, 2009.

'A guide to lower surgery for those assigned female, identifying as men, trans masculine, non-binary or non-gender,' GIRES 2015. Available at www.gires.org.uk/assets/Support-Assets/lower-surgery.pdf

Hung Jury: Testimonies of Genital Surgery by Transsexual Men, edited by Trystan T. Cotten, Transgress Press, 2012.

'Lower surgery for those assigned male, who identify as trans women, trans feminine, non-binary or non-gender,' GIRES, 2016. Available at www.gires.org.uk/assets/Support-Assets/lowersurgery-transwomen.pdf

'Management of the transgender adolescent,' by Olson, Forbes and Belzer, *Archives of Pediatric Adolescent Medicine 165*, 2, 171–176, 2011.

'Reproductive options for trans people,' Rainbow Health Ontario. Available at www.rainbowhealthontario.ca/resources/rho-fact-sheet-reproductive-options-for-trans-people

'Serving transgender youth: challenges, dilemmas, and clinical examples,' by Tishelman *et al.*, *Professional Psychology: Research and Practice 46*, 1, 37–45, 2015.

'Surgical Transition,' by Jules Chyten-Brennan, in *Trans Bodies, Trans Selves* (edited by Laura Erickson-Schroth), Oxford University Press, 2014.

'Young adult psychological outcome after puberty suppression and gender reassignment,' by de Vries *et al.*, *Pediatrics 134*, 4, 696–704, 2014.

CHAPTER 10

Referral for Medical Interventions

Most of the medical transition steps described in Chapter 9 require a referral from a mental health clinician. Some require two. Providing the evaluation of readiness for medical intervention is often described as the 'gatekeeper role.' This process is better viewed as an extension of the gender identity evaluation. It is a shared exploration of the young person's gender identity, in this case leading to a decision about whether a certain medical intervention, desired by the youth, is an appropriate next step in their gender transition. For those under the legal age of consent, the referral requires parental agreement in addition to the clinician's referral.

To make referrals, clinicians must find out who the experienced transgender health care practitioners are in their area, and how youth and families can access their services. The easiest way to find out is to ask other mental health clinicians with significant transgender experience. If you do not know who the experienced clinicians are in your area, take a look at the health information resources in Appendix B. Once you have a client who is questioning gender identity or expressing a transgender identity, it is good to begin this research, even if the youth has not yet requested a referral. It is helpful to have some time to talk to others about their experiences with practitioners or to contact the medical providers directly, all in advance of making a referral.

Of the medical transition steps listed in the previous chapter, here are the ones that generally require referral by a mental health clinician:

- puberty blockers
- cross-sex hormones
- top surgery
- hysterectomy and orchiectomy
- genital reconstruction surgery (GRS).

The criteria for making these referrals are outlined in the World Professional Association for Transgender Health (WPATH) *Standards of Care (SOC)*. (See 'For further exploration' at the end of this chapter to get a copy of the *SOC*.) Cross-sex hormones may also be accessed in some settings without a referral letter. This approach is often called 'informed consent.' I will discuss this further in the section on cross-sex hormone therapy. Another exception may be made in the case of a hysterectomy that is desired for gender transition but is also needed for medical reasons. In that instance the surgeon may not require a letter.

PUBERTY BLOCKERS

Puberty blocker treatment for transgender youth entering puberty was first offered at the Amsterdam Clinic for Children and Adolescents in 2000, and in the United States at Boston Children's Hospital beginning in 2007 (Spack *et al.* 2012). Since that time this treatment has been provided at hospitals, health centers and in private practice offices across the United States and elsewhere. According to the WPATH *SOC*:

> Two goals justify intervention with puberty-suppressing hormones: (i) their use gives adolescents more time to explore their gender nonconformity and other developmental issues and (ii) their use may facilitate transition by preventing the

development of sex characteristics that are difficult or impossible to reverse if adolescents continue on to pursue sex reassignment. (Coleman *et al.* 2011, p.177)

Puberty blockers are used primarily for youth who have attained a high level of certainty about their gender identity by the onset of puberty. But they are also used for those who are questioning their gender identity as they enter puberty and are distressed about missing this opportunity should they eventually gain certainty of a cross-gender identity. Therefore, uncertainty about gender identity does not rule out puberty suppression. Rather, it is expected to be present for some of the youths who are offered this treatment. According to Olson *et al.* (2011, p.175): 'Ideally, adolescents should be treated early [with blockers] to facilitate psychotherapy by easing distress, "buy time" to avoid reactive depression, and prevent unwanted secondary sex characteristics, thereby reducing the need for future medical interventions.'

As a result, there will be some who later discontinue puberty blockers and do not continue with cross-sex hormone therapy or gender transition. This may include those who during their time on blockers have affirmed a cisgender identity as well as those who have affirmed a non-binary identity and are comfortable resuming the progress of their innate puberty. Thus:

Puberty-delaying hormone treatment should not be viewed as a first step that inevitably leads to gender transition, but as a diagnostic aid. Therefore, 'real life experience' [social transition] is not required prior to or during hormonal treatment at this stage. (de Vries *et al.* 2006, p.91)

The important point is that in all cases, everyone involved (youth, parents, mental health and medical providers) gains time to sort out what is best for this youth and achieve as much certainty as possible before the youth continues with irreversible changes of their innate puberty or of cross-sex hormone therapy. In either case they do not have to grapple with unwanted changes that would have come with the wrong (for them) puberty. Before making a referral for puberty blockers, it is helpful to be in contact with the youth's primary care practitioner, with the youth and the family's permission, to discuss the assessment and treatment plan.

The specific criteria listed in the *SOC* for puberty-suppressing hormones include a longstanding history of gender non-conformance or dysphoria and an indication that gender dysphoria began or became worse at the start of puberty. Informed consent from the youth and parents or guardians is required. Any health, mental health or situational problems that could interfere with adherence to treatment need to be addressed in advance (Coleman *et al.* 2011).

It may seem that the first criterion above excludes the youth who is distressed or highly anxious about puberty and is just recently questioning gender identity. I advocate for allowing this youth access to blockers, since the alternative is pubertal change that will only increase the youth's distress and make it more difficult to carry out a thorough gender identity evaluation. In the end the youth could reach gender certainty with regret about the pubertal changes that occurred while they were sorting things out. Thus, it may turn out to be a badly missed opportunity. The guidelines in the *SOC* are intended to be flexible: 'The criteria...are clinical guidelines; individual health professionals and programs may modify them... The *SOC* articulate standards of care but also acknowledge the role of making informed choices and the value of harm-reduction approaches' (Coleman *et al.* 2011, pp.166–7).

A number of my teen clients were in mid- to late puberty when they realized their gender differed from the direction of their innate puberty. They were highly distressed about this and sought immediate hormone treatment to forestall further feminization or masculinization. Neither their parents nor I were comfortable recommending irreversible medical treatment without a thorough evaluation, but we appreciated that the youth's innate puberty would also bring irreversible changes, and these changes were more likely to turn out to be discordant than the ones that would come with cross-sex hormone therapy.

In these instances I have referred families for consultation with an endocrinologist who is experienced with puberty blocker treatment and the complicated questions that arise regarding offering it to youth who are no longer in the early stages of puberty. An evaluation by an experienced medical practitioner can clarify which of the remaining changes of puberty may be prevented by initiation of puberty blockers at that point, whether there are medical risks such as reduced bone density, and whether simultaneous administration of low-dose cross-sex hormones would reduce these risks while creating only minimal cross-sex changes. The goal is to allow the youth time to explore gender identity in therapy without panic, despair or disturbing physical changes. These are complex medical decisions. This scenario demonstrates the importance of identifying medical resources as soon as you are aware that your teen or young adult client is grappling with gender identity questions.

CROSS-SEX HORMONES

As discussed above, the effects of puberty blockers have so far been shown to be reversible for youth who discontinue them without transitioning to cross-sex hormones. But treatment with cross-sex hormone therapy has permanent as well as reversible effects, even after just a few months of use. Therefore, we expect a youth to reach a high level of certainty before beginning treatment with estrogen or testosterone. This is achieved by a combination of self-reflection, discussion with family and friends, counseling and, if possible, social transition. While I mentioned in Chapter 9 that the first few weeks of hormone treatment may serve as the final confirmation of this certainty, a high degree of clarity on the youth's part should be in place before referring for hormones. Often the social transition and the early response to hormone therapy serve to help the parents and the clinician feel sure, rather than the youth, who may have felt certain all along.

The *SOC* provide four criteria for cross-sex hormone treatment. The primary one is 'persistent, well-documented gender dysphoria.' The second is informed consent. Third, it is expected that the individual has reached the age of majority in their locality. Finally, any health or mental health concerns 'must be reasonably well-controlled' (Coleman *et al.* 2011, p.187).

For youth under the age of consent, the reader is referred to Section VI of the *SOC*, which states:

> Adolescents may be eligible to begin feminizing/masculinizing hormone therapy, preferably with parental consent. In many countries, 16-year-olds are legal adults for medical decision-making and do not require parental consent. Ideally, treatment decisions should be made among the adolescent, the family, and the treatment team... Refusing timely medical interventions for adolescents might prolong gender dysphoria and contribute to an appearance that could provoke abuse and stigmatization... [W]ithholding puberty-suppression and subsequent feminizing or masculinizing hormone therapy is not a neutral option for adolescents. (Coleman *et al.* 2011, p.178)

The criteria cited in the previous section of this chapter, for puberty blockers, turn out to be useful as well in consideration of adolescent readiness for cross-sex hormones. And while hormone treatment at age 16 is recommended by the Endocrine Society (Hembree *et al.* 2009), and has been customary at some of the centers that treat transgender youth, waiting until age 16 for a teen who has affirmed their transgender identity at age 15 or younger may not be in the child's best interest. Olson *et al.* state:

> It is often not pragmatic to delay the initiation of treatment with cross-gender hormones until the patient becomes 16 years of age. Delay can lead to similar emotional concerns that have been associated with constitutional delay of puberty. While this approach is unstudied, we advocate using age 16 as a guideline

and consider the earlier initiation of cross-gender hormones on a case-by-case basis after careful review of the potential risks and benefits with the youth and parents. Ultimately, the objective of medical treatment is appropriate masculinization or feminization of patients. (Olson *et al.* 2011, p.175)

Amy Ellis Nutt describes a decision to start cross-sex hormones for a 13-year-old who was previously on puberty blockers (2015). Stephen Rosenthal writes that he and his colleagues at the University of California, San Francisco:

...are studying the impact of cross-sex hormone treatment initiation at 14 years of age (which approximates the upper end of the age range for normal pubertal onset in natal males and 1 year beyond the upper end of the age range in natal females). (Rosenthal 2014, p.4385)

Similarly, Diane Chen and her colleagues in Chicago (2016) mention 14 as an age when many transgender youth are cognitively and emotionally ready for cross-sex hormones. These writings reflect the idea that the best experience for transgender youth would be to experience puberty in their affirmed gender at the same time their peers are entering puberty, if this can be accomplished safely and with certainty about the youth's affirmed gender. Laura Finken, in a review of research on age and decision making, concludes that 'by middle adolescence (approximately ages 14–15), the basic cognitive components for competent decision making seem to have developed' (2009, p.13).

Criteria 1 and 3: Documentation of persistent gender dysphoria; age of majority

The documentation of gender dysphoria is your written record of the gender identity evaluation. Regarding 'persistence,' the *SOC* do not offer a specific time frame. This allows experienced clinicians to rely on their expertise when making decisions about readiness and avoids unfair exclusion based on a rigid time requirement. Less experienced clinicians benefit from time-based suggestions. The *DSM-5* requires the duration of Gender Dysphoria indicators to be at least six months, making no distinction in this regard between adolescents and adults (American Psychiatric Association 2013). Version 6 of the *SOC* (Meyer, III *et al.* 2005), which was the most current one when I began doing this work, suggested six months of therapy and social transition prior to referring for hormone therapy. I found that suggestion helpful when I had little experience of my own to rely on.

When I look back on records from my earliest treatment of transgender youth, I see that I took much longer to reach certainty about medical referrals than I did after years of experience. The youth I worked with in those days, even if they were anxious to transition, accepted that longer time frame. They realized that the opportunity to transition as a teen was a benefit many of their peers did not have. Often their parents were highly reluctant to proceed with medical intervention, and the teens needed to come to terms with the idea that getting their parents on board could be a lengthy process. In more recent years, many families arrived at my office with both the teen or young adult and the parents feeling a relatively high degree of certainty about the youth's transgender identity and need for medical intervention. This has put me at times in the position of having to slow things down a bit, while making sure not to lose valuable time if the teen was in the middle of an unwanted puberty and upset about any further physical changes in that direction.

When I train and supervise mental health clinicians who are new to this work, I realize they need some sense of a timeline for authorizing medical interventions with confidence. I also find a timeline is helpful for parents who fear that their child is too young or is moving too quickly through this process. I have found it helpful to suggest the following:

1. In light of the research that exists for gender identity persistence and successful psychosocial outcomes for youth who transition with cross-sex hormones starting at age 16 (de Vries *et al.* 2014), and the shared experience among practitioners that most transgender youth seeking treatment have a firm sense of their gender identity younger than that, I believe that a clinician can be confident that a youth who is 15 or older and is without significant intellectual or social deficits can be certain of their gender identity.

2. Look for indications in the youth's reported history that:
   a. at least two years prior to referral for medical intervention the youth had some sense of gender discordance, perhaps not clearly articulated at the time but in retrospect continuous with their current feelings of gender discordance
   b. the youth has been talking to someone (friend, parent, clinician, etc.) for at least a year about feelings of gender discordance, and has experienced certainty about their gender identity for at least six months
   c. the youth has had an evaluation of gender identity over a period of three to six months and, if possible and safe, a social transition of three to six months. These two processes can overlap in time.

3. Make sure that the youth has done some research on their own and/or has asked detailed questions in therapy about the medical treatment they are seeking.

Adjustments to these time guidelines would include the following:

1. Take more time with youth who:
   a. are younger than age 15
   b. have a non-binary gender identity, which leads to more complex decisions about medical intervention and may reflect a gender identity in flux

    c. have had recent mental health or substance use difficulties that could interfere with current stability, self-understanding or ability to adhere to medical treatment

    d. have been diagnosed with an autism spectrum disorder

    e. are intellectually limited

    f. have had little interaction with others about their gender identity.

2. Consider moving more quickly with youth who are in tremendous distress about their gender discordance, especially those at risk of self-harm or suicide.

3. Consider a referral for discussion of the benefits and risks of puberty blockers if more time is needed for the evaluation and the youth is in distress about ongoing pubertal changes.

4. Recognize that youth who are heading to college may benefit from starting hormone therapy early in their final year of high school to allow for significant changes by the time they arrive at college.

Criterion 2: Informed consent

For teens under the legal age of consent, the informed consent process must include the teen and their parents or guardian. Keep in mind that the biological parents of a youth in foster care may not have surrendered their parental rights. For some youth, a Guardian Ad Litem[1] has been appointed and is in charge of medical decisions. Others live with grandparents or other relatives, but the parents retain legal custody. In all instances, it is essential to know who the significant adults are in the young person's life, both emotionally and legally. For youth above the age of consent, I recommend including the parents or guardians when possible, as they continue to play an important role in the lives of most young adults.

---

1   A Guardian Ad Litem is a person appointed by the court to determine what decisions are in the best interests of the child, including but not limited to custody, visitation, health and education.

The informed consent process for medical intervention happens in two parts, first in the office of the mental health clinician, and then in more detail at the physician's office. Most mental health clinicians assisting transgender youth are not medically trained. Our role is to share the information we have about the benefits and risks of the medical treatment and to encourage the family to review the same information with the medical provider and ask the provider any questions they have about the intervention. It has been my practice to work from the information tables in the *SOC* (Coleman *et al.* 2011, pp.188–190), with additional discussion of fertility and possible impact on mood, as discussed in Chapter 9 of this book. Other good sources of information on hormone treatment are listed at the end of this chapter.

Olson *et al.* summarize the primary benefits and risks as follows:

Administration of cross-gender hormones in transgender female patients would be expected to induce breast growth (irreversible), change body fat composition (reversible), and decrease facial and body hair (reversible). Adverse effects might include development of deep venous thrombophlebitis,[2] prolactinoma,[3] hypertension, liver disease, decreased libido, and increased risk of breast cancer. Androgen blockers can cause hyperkalemia[4] and decreased blood pressure. Most transgender females receiving cross-gender hormones will experience a decrease in testicular mass, penis size, and fertility (irreversible)...

The administration of testosterone in transgender male patients will induce a drop in the voice, clitoral enlargement ([both] irreversible), facial and body hair growth, cessation of menses, redistribution of fat (all reversible), and increase in

---

2   Deep vein thrombosis, or DVT, is caused by a blood clot in a deep vein and can be life-threatening.

3   A prolactinoma is a benign tumor that grows on the pituitary gland and makes too much prolactin.

4   Hyperkalemia is too much potassium in the blood, which can lead to dangerous changes in heart rhythm.

lean muscle mass (reversible). Potential adverse effects might include hyperlipidemia,[5] polycythemia,[6] male pattern baldness (if a genetic predisposition exists), acne, and infertility. (Olson *et al.* 2011, p.175)

I recommend that you contact the youth's primary care practitioner, with the youth and the family's permission, to discuss the referral for cross-sex hormones, especially if this is to be the first gender-related medical intervention for this youth. Parents and youth also need to know the importance of lifelong follow-up with whoever is prescribing their hormone treatment:

Adolescents undergoing cross-gender hormone therapy need ongoing care, including monitoring for potential medical complications as well as an assessment of success in masculinization or feminization. In the first year of therapy, patients should be monitored every 3 months, particularly while their hormone dosages are being adjusted, to maximize desired effects and minimize negative effects. If patients achieve stability in their dosing regimen and the transitioning process is progressing adequately, they can be monitored less often. More frequent monitoring should be considered in patients who are younger or have medical or mental health conditions that might be exacerbated by cross-gender hormone use. (Olson *et al.* 2011, pp.175–6)

Criterion 4: Addressing any medical or mental health problems

While the *SOC* do not specify what they mean when they state that these problems must be 'reasonably controlled,' we can borrow the

---

5   The term hyperlipidemia covers several disorders that result in extra fats, also known as lipids, in the blood.
6   Polycythemia is an increase in the number of red blood cells.
    The medical definitions in footnotes 2–6 are from www.webmd.com (accessed on 11/21/2016), except for 'polycythemia,' which is from www.medicinenet.com (accessed on 3/19/2017).

third criterion for puberty blocker treatment, that 'any coexisting psychological, medical or social problems that could interfere with treatment (e.g., that may compromise treatment adherence) have been addressed, such that the adolescent's situation and functioning are stable enough to start treatment' (Coleman *et al.* 2011, p.177). This guideline allows us to hold off when there are safety concerns, but does not rule out needed treatment for youth who are still grappling with mental health challenges and symptoms. Often these symptoms will not resolve or improve until after the needed gender transition treatment is begun.

In my view there are only a few mental health conditions that rule out referral for medical interventions. The most obvious is active psychosis. While this has not been present for any of my clients, I would certainly not attempt an evaluation of gender identity with a client who is actively psychotic. Once the psychosis is treated and the youth is stable, the evaluation can proceed with a referral at the appropriate time. The *DSM-5* notes that even in individuals who have previously been diagnosed with schizophrenia or another psychotic disorder, affirmation of transgender identity in the absence of active psychosis is not considered delusional (American Psychiatric Association 2013).

It is important to note that the one cluster of psychiatric conditions mentioned in the *SOC* as at risk of destabilization with hormone treatment 'includes bipolar, schizoaffective and other disorders that may include manic or psychotic symptoms. This adverse event appears to be associated with higher doses or supraphysiologic blood levels of testosterone' (Coleman *et al.* 2011, p.190). Youth with a prior history of these disorders, or with a family history of bipolar disorder, should be carefully monitored by all of their medical and mental health providers, including anyone providing psychiatric medication, after starting treatment with testosterone.

There are no mental health conditions listed in the *SOC* as at risk of exacerbation by treatment with estrogen. Madeline Deutsch (2016) reports that 'there is no clear evidence that estrogen therapy is directly associated with the onset of or worsening of mental health conditions.' In fact, when viewed more broadly, treatment with cross-sex hormones has been shown to improve mental health in FTM and MTF transgender people (Gómez-Gil *et al.* 2012; Meier *et al.* 2011).

Substance use that interferes with functioning is another reason to delay medical intervention. Treatment can proceed once the problem is reasonably well controlled. In addition, youth and families need to know that tobacco use increases the risk of blood clots for individuals taking estrogen for gender transition. Tobacco use should be curtailed prior to treatment, but under the harm-reduction model it is not an absolute barrier to hormone therapy (Deutsch 2014; Deutsch 2016).

One additional reason to delay medical transition, in my view, is complete social isolation, or when socializing is limited to online contacts. In the course of my work with transgender youth I have come to see the immense value of the information and support provided by youth interacting with other transgender youth and adults online. Nonetheless, I feel strongly that youth undertaking irreversible medical intervention should have some experience interacting with others in person in their affirmed gender. Most often this will occur in the family context or at school, even if on a very part-time basis. For those who are too socially anxious to do so at school, or who have a school and family environment that does not provide a venue for safe expression, I work with the youth on identifying some peers or adults with whom they can safely spend time expressing their affirmed gender. In most instances we have been able to accomplish this goal as part of the gender identity evaluation prior to medical referral.

Any discussion of the benefits and risks of hormone therapy must include consideration of the risk of denying this treatment to a youth who desperately wants it and fears what life will be like if medical intervention does not start soon. One significant risk is that the youth will seek hormones or supplements from non-medical sources, in their community or online, and be in danger. Catherine Holman and Joshua Goldberg describe this risk:

> Estrogen and testosterone can be purchased illicitly or through the internet, or shared among friends. The risks associated with cross-sex hormones are exponentially increased when there is no screening for health conditions that may be made worse by hormone use, or regular medical monitoring of adverse effects after hormones are started (Dahl, Feldman, Goldberg and Jaberi 2006). Non-prescription-grade hormones may be poor quality and may be diluted with toxic substances. For those taking hormones by injection, improper injection technique or needle sharing poses additional health hazards such as abscess and transmission of HIV and Hepatitis C. (Holman and Goldberg 2006, p.107)

The goal is to proceed carefully, exercise reasonable caution and be attentive to the intensely felt need of many transgender youth to move ahead with medical intervention in as timely a manner as possible.

> The ability to provide optimal health care to gender-dysphoric/ transgender youth is limited by areas of uncertainty, controversies, and barriers to state-of-the art practice. Only limited safety and efficacy data currently exist, with virtually no published data on the use of pubertal blockers in gender-dysphoric individuals [less than] 12 years of age or cross-sex hormones in transgender youth [less than] 16 years of age... The clinical practice guidelines that currently exist are based on best available evidence, with significant reliance on expert opinion. (Rosenthal 2014, p.4387)

THE 'INFORMED CONSENT' MODEL FOR YOUTH 18 AND OLDER

Some community health centers providing services for the transgender community offer hormone therapy on the basis of what is often referred to as the 'informed consent' model. In these centers, the prescriber or another trained staff member carries out the evaluation of readiness including discussion of hormone benefits and risks, before providing the requested treatment. A prior evaluation and referral by a mental health practitioner is not required. One such protocol states:

> Prescribing hormones is at the discretion of the medical provider and is based on medical history, physical exam, lab test results and review of nursing and psycho-social assessments. A patient's ability to give informed consent is required prior to starting treatment. At times if there is a question of a patient's ability to give informed consent further evaluation may be necessary. Willingness to enter into comprehensive primary health care and keeping appointments is also required. (Tom Waddell Health Center 2013)

In this particular protocol, hormones are not prescribed at the first visit.

A 2009 survey of 12 sites in the United States that offer hormone therapy on an informed consent basis reviewed protocols and outcomes (Deutsch 2013). Only a third of the centers reported mental health clinician involvement during the intake process. Patient outcomes were good and regrets were rare. Hormone therapy at these centers is an option for young adults who are certain of their gender identity and do not feel a need for counseling prior to seeking treatment.

TOP SURGERY

The criteria listed in the *SOC* for top surgery are identical to those for cross-sex hormone therapy: documentation of persistent gender dysphoria; informed consent; age of majority; and that any medical or mental health problems are 'reasonably well controlled' (Coleman *et al.* 2011, p.201). Hormone therapy is not a prerequisite for top surgery, although it usually precedes top surgery for youth.

Regarding top surgery for youth who have not reached the age of majority, the *SOC* state in Section VI:

> Chest surgery in FtM patients could be carried out earlier, preferably after ample time of living in the desired gender role and after one year of testosterone treatment. The intent of this suggested sequence is to give adolescents sufficient opportunity to experience and socially adjust in a more masculine gender role, before undergoing irreversible surgery. However, different approaches may be more suitable, depending on an adolescent's specific clinical situation and goals for gender identity expression. (Coleman *et al.* 2011, p.178)

When possible, wearing a binder and carrying out a social transition are helpful steps for confirmation that top surgery is right for a youth who is transitioning from female to a male or non-binary identity. If top surgery is the first medical intervention being sought, the same caveats about timing for cross-sex hormone therapy apply (see the discussion earlier in the chapter about cross-sex hormone treatment). A youth who has already been undergoing masculinization with hormones for 6–12 months, has been living full time as male or not-female, and has continuously expressed an interest in top surgery is likely to be ready for this step, but the same precautions should be taken as are discussed in the section on cross-sex hormone therapy above. The timetable may be accelerated for a youth with a very high level of distress regarding their female chest, or for a youth who is six months or less away from going to college. Generally, trans youth seeking top surgery who are high school seniors would like to have their surgery and a few weeks of recovery completed at least a month before going to college.

Informed consent for top surgery includes awareness of: the risks of surgery; the choices among types of top surgery, which can result in different outcomes; the possible need for a surgical revision; and the length and physical limitations of the recovery from surgery. Most young people that I worked with researched this information online, often at the websites of surgeons who are highly experienced in the surgery they were seeking. Youths and their parents will have a consultation with the surgeon in advance of scheduling the surgery. This is an opportunity to learn detailed information about surgical options as well as possible risks and outcomes, and to ask questions. There are resources listed at the end of this chapter and the previous chapter that provide surgery information.

HYSTERECTOMY, ORCHIECTOMY AND GENITAL RECONSTRUCTION SURGERY

As interventions for gender transition, the primary purposes of hysterectomy and orchiectomy are to reduce the body's endogenous production of unwanted sex hormones, and to remove organs that do not align with the individual's gender identity. Genital reconstruction surgery (GRS) is much more extensive surgery, which may include hysterectomy or orchiectomy but also serves to alter the appearance and functioning of the genitalia to be in accordance with the individual's affirmed gender identity. The procedures that may be included in GRS are listed in Chapter 9.

The *SOC* specify that two referral letters are required for all of these surgeries. Only one letter is required for hormone therapies and top surgery. Version 6 of the *SOC* required that if 'the first letter is from a person with a master's degree, the second letter should be from a psychiatrist or a Ph.D. clinical psychologist' (Meyer, III *et al.* 2005, p.14). Many insurers have retained this requirement, even though it was dropped from the most current *SOC*. I have also encountered one insurer that required two letters for top surgery. It is important for individuals seeking insurance coverage for surgery to request a copy of their insurance plan's requirements, as these may differ from the criteria in the *SOC* that I will be discussing here. They should also find out if the surgeon's requirements differ in any way from the *SOC*.

The first four criteria for hysterectomy (removal of the uterus), salpingo-oophorectomy (removal of the fallopian tubes and ovaries) and orchiectomy (removal of the testicles) are the same four criteria listed for top surgery: documentation of persistent gender dysphoria; informed consent; age of majority; and that any medical or mental health problems are 'reasonably well controlled.' There is one additional criterion, listed as number 5: '12 continuous months of hormone therapy as appropriate to the patient's gender goals (unless hormones are not clinically indicated for the individual)' (Coleman *et al*. 2011, p.202).

For metoidioplasty, phalloplasty and vaginoplasty (the procedures to create genitals concordant with gender identity), the *SOC* add a sixth criterion: '12 continuous months of living in a gender role that is congruent with the patient's identity' (Coleman *et al*. 2011, p.202). The *SOC* present the following rationale for requiring 12 months of living in a congruent gender role:

> Changing gender role can have profound personal and social consequences, and the decision to do so should include an awareness of what the familial, interpersonal, educational, vocational, economic, and legal challenges are likely to be, so that people can function successfully in their gender role... The duration of 12 months allows for a range of different life experiences and events that may occur throughout the year (e.g., family events, holidays, vacations, season-specific work or school experiences). During this time, patients should present consistently, on a day-to-day basis and across all settings of life, in their desired gender role. (Coleman *et al*. 2011, p.202)

The period of living full time in the affirmed gender is believed to give the person the best view of what the future may hold. This, in turn, allows for even greater certainty about the decision to undergo complex and irreversible surgery or, in many cases, more than one surgery. During this year the individual will also have ample time to research procedures, surgeons, risks and outcomes.

While the criteria for genital surgeries include the requirement that the individual has reached the age of majority, which can be as low as 16 in some countries, 18 remains the most common age at which surgeons will provide this surgery. Christine Milrod (2014, p.342) notes: 'By imposing the 18-year age threshold for irreversible genital procedures, the available ethical standards aim to balance the suffering of the waiting adolescent with avoiding the risk of postsurgery regret.' Currently some surgeons and hospitals in the United States will consider an MTF patient at age 17 for GRS (Milrod 2014). Access to genital surgery is limited by the following factors: cost; the relatively small number of experienced surgeons, some with waiting lists of a year or more; ability to travel to an experienced surgeon; insurance coverage; having a support person to help before and after surgery; and having favorable life circumstances for recovery. The latter is especially true for phalloplasty, which involves multiple procedures, and vaginoplasty, which requires repeated dilation afterward, initially multiple times per day.

Milrod (2014) examines the ethics of allowing genital surgery for transgender female-affirmed youth under 18 years of age. She points out that for youth who have already transitioned socially and who are not known by their peers to be transgender, genital incongruence can lead to fears of discovery, loss of privacy and subsequent harassment or violence. These fears lead to guardedness that can impair friendships and other relationships. In addition, these teens experience many obstacles to age-typical dating, romance and sexual exploration due to their genital differences. Milrod provides ethical guidelines derived from those established for managing the care of children with disorders of sexual development. She highlights four principles (paraphrased here):

1. psychological support and education for the youth and her parents or guardians, provided by a mental health practitioner knowledgeable about transgender identity development and relevant medical interventions

2. explanation of the surgical procedure for the youth and her parents or guardians by the surgeon, with full disclosure of risks, variations in outcome and postoperative management
3. assessment by the medical and mental health professionals of the risks of surgery versus the psychosocial risks of delaying surgery that the youth strongly desires
4. the adolescent's right to privacy and to final consent regarding her body. Certainty that the teen is providing full, free and informed consent, and confidence that she is as competent to do so as someone who is 18 years old.

Informed consent for these surgeries includes awareness of the risks of surgery, the choices among types of genital surgery and their different outcomes, the possible need for multiple surgeries and/or surgical revision, and the length and physical limitations of the recovery from surgery. Most young people that I worked with researched this information online, often at the websites of the surgeons who are highly experienced in genital surgery. The initial consultation with the surgeon is an opportunity to learn detailed information about their particular surgical options as well as possible risks and outcomes, and to ask questions. (See the resources listed at the end of this chapter and at the end of Chapter 9 that provide surgery information.)

Generally the surgical practice will require referral letters prior to the initial consultation, or the insurance company may require them to cover payment for the consultation, so the mental health clinician's validation of informed consent includes an awareness that the individual has gathered information about the surgery they are seeking and plans to ask further, detailed questions when they meet with the surgeon.

WRITING REFERRAL LETTERS

Below is my outline for letters regarding readiness for medical intervention. These are suggestions for what should be included in the letter, with a recommended sequence for the information. Feel free to alter the format and content as you see fit. When in doubt about how a client may feel about what you have written, it is best to discuss the content of the letter with your client before sending it.

1. Introduction and identifying data:
   a. The purpose of the letter (recommending evaluation by the medical provider for hormones or surgery).
   b. The client's legal name at the start and end of the letter; otherwise use affirmed name and pronouns. Client's age. Brief description of their gender identity.
   c. The clinician's experience with gender identity evaluations.
   d. The *DSM-5* Diagnosis (F64.1, Gender Dysphoria; plus additional mental health diagnoses, if any).
2. Developmental history highlighting gender identity awareness; gender expression; gender identity disclosure and responses; any medical, mental health or substance abuse history and treatment.
3. Duration of your professional relationship with this client; number of sessions; inclusion of significant others; contact with other mental health or medical providers.
4. Client's goals for medical intervention. Your agreement that this is an appropriate next step in their transition. If you are aware of any medical concerns, include them in the letter, even though the treating physician will take a complete medical history.
5. Statement that the client meets the *SOC*: the client is mentally stable (intellectually competent and any mental health or substance abuse problems are being addressed); is able to make an informed decision and give consent; if under the age of majority in your country, that the parents have given consent; for GRS, that time requirements have been met.
6. State that in your opinion this treatment is necessary for the client's well-being.

7. Recommendations for ongoing mental health care, and/or to follow up with you on an as-needed basis.
8. Your availability should the medical provider have any questions about your recommendation.

You will find sample referral letters in Appendix C.

FOR FURTHER EXPLORATION

Information on hormone effects

'Medical Transition,' by Maddie Deutsch, in *Trans Bodies, Trans Selves* (edited by Laura Erickson-Schroth), Oxford University Press, 2014.

'Overview of feminizing hormone therapy' and 'Overview of masculinizing hormone therapy,' by Maddie Deutsch. Search for each article by title at: www.transhealth.ucsf.edu.

'Physical aspects of transgender endocrine therapy,' by Marshall Dahl *et al.*, *International Journal of Transgenderism 9*, 3/4, 111–134, 2006.

World Professional Association for Transgender Health (WPATH), *Standards of Care for the Health of Transsexual, Transgender, and Gender Nonconforming People*, pages 188–90. Find it at www.wpath.org under Publications/ Standards of Care. In the right-hand column click on the language you prefer. You can get a free PDF download or purchase a print copy.

Information on surgeries

'Care of the patient undergoing sex reassignment surgery,' by Cameron Bowman and Joshua Goldberg, *International Journal of Transgenderism 9*, 3/4, 135–65, 2006. This article includes detailed information on all of the surgeries discussed in this chapter, not just GRS.

See, also, the surgery resources at the end of Chapter 9.

Article on ethics

'How young is too young: Ethical concerns in genital surgery of the transgender MTF adolescent,' by Christine Milrod, *Journal of Sexual Medicine 11*, 2, 338–46, 2014.

Other outlines for writing referral letters

'How to Write a Letter for Hormones or Surgery,' by Kit Rachlin, on page 299 in *Trans Bodies, Trans Selves* (edited by Laura Erickson-Schroth), Oxford University Press, 2014.

Recommended content of the referral letter is described in the WPATH *Standards of Care* (pages 182 and 183). See above for instructions for getting a copy of the *SOC*.

See also the websites of surgeons who provide gender affirmation surgeries for a description of what they want you to include in your letter.

YOUTH IN CONTEXT

CHAPTER 11

Family Therapy

In *Far From the Tree*, Andrew Solomon (2012) points out that children who suffer harassment or discrimination based on race, religion or socioeconomic status generally have parents who have experienced the same challenges. They get validation from their family for who they are despite the negative views that may exist in their community. They receive guidance about how to respond safely to harassment, and support to counter anguish and rage when not feeling safe to respond. This helps them develop self-esteem even in the face of disrespect from others.

Transgender youth most likely do not have parents or any extended family members who are transgender. As with other youth whose stigmatized status is not shared by their family, their parents are not able to offer an insider's view on how to cope with these challenges. Parents, in fact, often feel completely unprepared to offer the support and guidance these children need. And many families are initially quite rejecting of their transgender young people.

The Family Acceptance Project (FAP) has demonstrated the impact of highly rejecting family responses on LGBT youth:

> Our research shows that gay and transgender youth who were rejected by their families because of their identity had much lower self-esteem. They had fewer people they could turn to for

help. And they were more isolated than youth who were accepted by their families. Gay and transgender teens who were highly rejected by their parents and caregivers were at very high risk for health and mental health problems when they become young adults (ages 21–25). (Ryan 2009, p.5)

The FAP found that rates of depression, suicide attempts, substance use and sexually transmitted diseases are three to eight times higher in LGBT youth with highly rejecting families when compared with LGBT youth whose families were accepting or only mildly rejecting.

The 2015 US Transgender Survey (National Center for Transgender Equality 2016) shows the same negative impact of unsupportive families on the well-being of transgender adults. And while peer relationships gain tremendous importance in adolescence, teens who are close to their parents engage in fewer risky behaviors (Finken 2009).

For these reasons, family therapy has an extremely important role in the assistance we offer transgender youth. Family therapy is a vehicle for altering rejecting behaviors as well as a way to help parents understand and advocate for their children. Many of the steps that transgender or questioning teens need to take require parental agreement. Other steps for teens, as well as those for young adults, may be accessed without parental support, but require greater effort and forbearance. Some trans youth not only lack active parental involvement but have also been rejected subtly or directly by their family for being gender nonconforming or transgender. They carry a heavy burden that weighs them down in the process of self-actualization and impedes their progress. For these young people, family therapy is key if it is at all possible.

Robb Travers and his colleagues in Ontario, Canada, surveyed transgender youth 16 years and older on the impact of parental support. They found that:

...trans youth who indicated their parents were strongly supportive of their gender identity and expression were significantly more likely (72%) to report being satisfied with their lives than those with parents who were not strongly supportive (33%). Also statistically significant, 70% of those with parents strongly supportive of their gender identity and expression reported positive mental health compared to 15% of those whose parents were not strongly supportive. (Travers *et al.* 2012, p.2)

Family therapy begins with the young person's drive to embrace and express their authentic self, and their parents' determination to proceed safely. Many teens arrive insisting they know exactly who they are and what they need. They are generally well informed about transgender identities and the relevant medical interventions. They are impatient to proceed. Parents are often shocked and confused. They have generally had little time to process this new information, while the teen has been mulling it over for months before telling them. Parents may have trouble believing that what their child is saying could be true. They fear for their child's safety. Parents are faced 'with two potentially opposing socialization tasks: allowing the child to unfold to be his or her healthiest and most authentic self; ensuring that the child is safe in the world' (Ehrensaft 2012, p.344).

The goals of family therapy are to improve communication and understanding, and to examine the urge for an authentic life as well as the safety concerns that arise with gender transition, while keeping in mind any risks from not transitioning. Family therapy includes a gender identity evaluation of the youth and discussion with the parents of their fears and concerns. Later in this chapter I will offer my suggestions for helping parents address their fears and concerns. By paying attention to both authenticity and safety, it is usually possible to reach a shared understanding between the youth, the parents and the therapist that guides any decisions moving forward.

GETTING STARTED

The purpose of the initial sessions is to get an overview of the presenting problems and goals for treatment, and to establish rapport with the youth and the parents or guardians. The presenting problems include those related to gender identity along with any other mental health or behavioral concerns raised by the youth or the parents. I aim to establish rapport by validating all of the concerns raised by the participants and explaining how we will address them over the course of treatment. I let the young person know that I understand their need for authenticity. I assure them that even if they are discouraged by their parents' initial response, they can feel hopeful because their parents are engaged in treatment. I assure the parents that I will provide an evaluation of gender identity and any mental health concerns, and that I am aware of the safety concerns that parents have.

Be careful to ally with the parents as well as with the youth, even if you disagree with many of the parents' ideas. Parents are likely to suspect, perhaps correctly, that you are biased against some of their views. Aim to be on everyone's side. You may find that it is easier to empathize with the youth's struggles. Make sure that you also give full attention to the parents' equally valid pain and fear. Look for shared concerns rather than just noticing disagreements. Emphasize the values of safety, authenticity, personal exploration and actualization. If the family's religious or cultural background does not support individuality and free expression, focus on safety and the dangers faced by transgender youth who lack family support.

Sometimes one parent supports while another challenges the validity of the child's expression of transgender identity. In these instances it is best to focus on connecting with the challenging parent. Validate this parent's concerns as safety concerns. Assure them that you will address all of their concerns in the course of your evaluation. Point out that everyone in the room wants to understand what is going on and wants to proceed in the child's best interest.

In cases of divorce, if the challenging parent is the one with primary custody or the one who tends to be more involved in childrearing and medical decisions, losing that parent may lead to an inability to help the child. Conflict between the parents may be part of the family's post-divorce structure. You should do all you can to avoid being seen as taking sides in this battle. Keep in mind that anything you say separately to either parent or to the child may be repeated to the others without your precise and nuanced choice of words. Focus on establishing rapport and a trusting relationship with the parent who is most distressed about or doubting of the child's transgender identity expression. It is unhelpful to create or perpetuate a situation in which the parent with greater concern or caution is characterized as the bad one.

To begin family therapy with teens under the age of 15 or pre-teens, I generally meet with the parents first. With older teens, I start with the teen and parents together, or with the young person alone, based on the young person's preference. For 18 and older I usually meet with the young adult alone first, unless they prefer to include their parents at the start. I emphasize to young adults that the outcome will be best with parental participation at some point, if that is available. But some young people have waited until they are 18 to proceed because they know or believe that their parents will be extremely hostile. They need to proceed cautiously if they are still dependent financially or emotionally on their parents.

While the course of treatment varies from family to family, here is a summary of how the initial family therapy sessions are structured:

- first session for parents only for youth under 15
- first session for parents and teen together for 15–17 years old
- first session for young adult alone if 18 or older
- conjoint session with youth and parents if initial session was not conjoint.

The goal of these sessions is for each member to feel engaged in the process and have their viewpoint acknowledged. In some families, not every parent is aware that the youth has expressed gender identity concerns. For these families, the initial sessions include the parents who know. One of the treatment goals will be figuring out how and when to inform the other parents.

STRUCTURE AND TASKS OF FAMILY THERAPY

After the initial session or two, family therapy proceeds with a few different processes occurring in tandem. The frequency and timing of the sessions will vary from family to family. The goal is to move each aspect of the process forward in a timely manner. Schedule conjoint family sessions to integrate information from the separate sessions and to address any obstacles to achieving a shared understanding of the youth's identity and their needs. The components of family therapy with transgender youth are:

- individual sessions for the young person
- sessions for the parents or guardians
- referral for ancillary mental health or substance abuse treatment
- conjoint sessions with the youth and parents or guardians together
- additional supports for the youth and family.

Individual sessions for the young person

The initial focus of the individual sessions is a full assessment of the youth's gender identity and mental health. The details of the gender identity evaluation are covered in Chapter 6. The mental health assessment is the same you would provide to any other teen or young adult, based on your experience and training as a mental health clinician. Keep in mind the interactions between trans identities and mental health discussed in Chapter 7. Address any urgent mental health problems immediately. Other mental health concerns are best addressed in the overall treatment plan that emerges from the assessment.

These sessions include discussion of any disclosure of gender identity to others, gender expression outside of cultural expectations, and the social transition if it has been initiated in part or in full. This is an opportunity for the youth to reflect on others' reactions and their own feelings in response. For youth who have disclosed their identity to few or no peers, we also talk about how it feels to be keeping this secret. All of these factors affect the young person's self-esteem and functioning. You can begin to address these issues as you conduct the evaluation (de Vries *et al.* 2006). Interventions include validating feelings, identifying societal biases that harm LGBT youth and strategizing about effective communication with significant others. Should any safety concerns arise, engage parents and other adults, such as school personnel, to provide safety.

Sessions for the parents or guardians
While most transgender youth seeking treatment are living with one or more parents, many are living with other relatives, in foster care or in group homes. In the latter instances I have found that social service workers assigned to these youth have been extremely supportive and open-minded about their needs. But this may not be the case for a transgender teen you are helping. Guardians other than parents may have many of the same fears and concerns that parents have. Family therapy that includes these adults is just as important for the youth in foster care, a group home or a relative's home as it is for a youth who resides with parents (National Clearinghouse on Families and Youth 2016b). When parents and youth are in more than one household, consider including other adults, such as the parents' partners or spouses or other relatives who have a parental role.

These sessions with the relevant adults have a number of goals. The first is to gather history for your evaluation of the youth, including both gender-related and other developmental and behavioral factors. Parents are more likely than youth to be able give an accurate description of prior medical and mental health treatment, as well as early life events and challenges.

The second goal is to provide the adults with the information they need to understand transgender identities in general. This will give them a context within which to understand their child. It is essential as part of the family therapy process to educate parents or guardians about transgender identity development and possible transition steps, including the value of social transition as a part of the evaluation. Be sure to point out to them that many transgender youth were gender conforming as children. When transgender identity seems to come from nowhere, parents find it especially difficult to believe. Let these parents know that puberty is a common time for youth to realize their transgender identity (Grossman and D'Augelli 2006).

The third goal is to help parents address their particular fears and concerns. My suggestions for doing so are given later in this chapter.

Sometimes parents are not able or not willing to attend the sessions together. In these instances it is important to meet with each parent who would like to participate, even if this requires extra meetings. When one or more of the parents are located elsewhere, phone calls can take the place of in-person sessions. Similarly, a conference call with the youth in your office and the parents on the phone can take the place of conjoint sessions, although I find in-person family sessions more effective. Family dynamics and emotions communicated through body language and facial expression are missed on the phone. This is less likely to be a problem when calling parents to get the history and hear their concerns.

For youth who are 18 and older, parental involvement is not a requirement for medical transition steps. But it is my belief that for 18–21-year-olds family sessions are almost as important as they are for 15–17-year-olds. Many young adults in 21st-century America continue to rely on their parents for advice and support. Establishing financial independence can be difficult in our current economy. Including parents so they can understand and support their transgender youth just makes sense. But young adults with strained family relationships are less likely to want to include their parents. For these youth and for those whose parents live at a great distance, parent participation tends to occur a bit later in the sequence of sessions.

With youth who are over the age of majority, the decision whether and how to include parents is ultimately theirs. It is up to the therapist to explain the benefits of including parents to the youth who is reluctant to do so. They may feel less reluctant once they are confident that you understand who they are and what they need. They will be less afraid that you will be swayed by any concerns raised by their parents.

Referral for ancillary mental health or substance abuse treatment

When the individual or parent sessions lead to an assessment of significant mental health concerns in addition to gender identity concerns, the treatment plan must address those problems. Treatment can occur within the therapy you are providing, or by referral to another clinician or program. Prior mental health treatment will also be a relevant factor, as the youth and family may have strong positive or negative feelings about returning to prior treaters. Your time availability and expertise with the specific mental health or substance abuse problem, as well as the youth and the family's preference for how to proceed, will all factor into this decision.

I do not recommend suspension of the gender identity evaluation and related family therapy except in cases of severe mental illness. Any delay should only be for the time needed to help the young person gain more stability and safety.

Conjoint sessions with the youth and parents or guardians together

After the introductory sessions, the next conjoint session generally occurs after your initial assessment is complete and the parents have had an opportunity to absorb information about transgender identities. A crisis, however, could lead to a conjoint session sooner. This happens more often than you might expect, as many youth are moving ahead with disclosures and more authentic gender expression without waiting for their parents to be ready. When the response is positive, the youth is generally fine; but when the youth's expression is viewed as transgressive by others and responses are negative, they may experience an emotional or situational crisis (such as harassment at school) that requires family discussion and intervention. It is important to be flexible in the scheduling of sessions and to vary the agenda as needed, based on events and the feelings expressed by the family members. Sometimes parents are anxious to hear more from their child, who may not be talking to them at home, so ongoing family meetings are needed to ease the parent's distress.

After completing the gender identity evaluation, I schedule a session or two for the youth to share their story with their parents. In those sessions the clinician helps the youth explain to the parents the substance of the gender identity evaluation: who they are, how they came to understand their gender identity, what distress they may be experiencing and what transition steps they may want to take. I find it helpful to interview the youth in front of the parents, asking questions about moments in their history that they have already shared with me. This helps the young person present a coherent narrative that makes sense to the parents.

In addition, I may interject some of my own thoughts along the way, or clarify language that is unclear to the parents. If the parents make comments or ask questions that come across as derogatory or dismissive, I try to help them find more supportive language that expresses their concerns. If the youth has requested that parents use a different name and pronouns, and the parents have been unwilling to do so, these sessions provide a good opportunity to talk about why this is so important for the youth. It may also be useful at this juncture to share some of the findings of the Family Acceptance Project (Ryan 2009). This information helps motivate parents to shift from rejecting to accepting viewpoints and behavior. For many parents I worked with, these sessions have been a turning point. They realized that their child was not using a transgender identity declaration to 'act out' or for other secondary gain.

Additional family sessions are scheduled as needed. At this point it is wise to include siblings if they are upset about their transgender sibling's transition or the effect it will have on them. Extended family members whose opinions matter to the parents can also be included if you believe that will help the family move forward. I have found it helpful to include family members who are more supportive than the parents, to help the parents feel more at ease. At other times we have invited in family members whose negative attitudes were affecting the youth or the parents, to see if I could help address their fears or concerns.

In-between, I continue meeting with the youth and offer separate meetings for the parents for each to reflect on what has been shared and prepare for future family meetings. Youth who feel their parents are listening to their gender concerns are more likely to listen to the parents' concerns about their mood, interactions and behaviors. These topics can then be addressed without rancor in family sessions. As it turns out, many of these other symptoms improve spontaneously once the youth feels validated, which in turn reassures the parents that the gender dysphoria is real.

Additional conjoint sessions are the forum for decisions about transition steps, such as additional disclosures, social transition and medical intervention. The informed consent discussions that precede any medical intervention should be conducted individually with the youth and then conjointly with the youth and the parents.

Additional supports for the youth and the family
Support groups can be a tremendous help for transgender youth. Sometimes these are available in the community. They may be provided at a local LGBT community center or by a therapist, life coach or youth advocate who specializes in working with transgender teens and young adults. A GSA (Gay Straight Alliance) at the child's school, while not limited to transgender peers, can be a valuable support. Many chapters of PFLAG (Parents and Friends of Lesbians and Gays) now provide a great deal of support to transgender individuals and their families. When there are no support groups in the area, families can attend a transgender youth conference to gain support and meet other families. See Appendix B for information about conferences and support organizations.

Parents and youth can keep in touch with families they meet at conferences. They can welcome peers from local support groups to visit their child at home and create opportunities for teens to spend time together socializing. Parents are reassured when they see their child spending time in typical ways with others their age.

ADDRESSING PARENTS' FEARS AND CONCERNS

The fears and concerns raised by parents in my practice have included the following:

- 'Our child is not really transgender.'
- 'Embracing transgender identity will lead to harassment or physical harm.'
- 'Our child will have an unhappy future as a transgender person.'
- 'Our child is too young. When they are older they will regret steps they take now.'
- 'There is no need to transition. People are no longer limited by gender.'
- 'This is happening too fast.'
- 'What did we do wrong?'
- 'This is embarrassing.'
- 'This is a loss for us.'

'Our child is not really transgender'

Some parents believe that their child's statement of transgender identity is a sign of mental illness or confusion. Or perhaps their child is just trying to upset them or fit in with a fringe group of peers. Sometimes it seems to parents, and perhaps to other adults, that the trans identity is a reaction to a loss or trauma in the young person's life.

In the separate sessions for the parents, as discussed above, you have established a foundation to help parents understand the reality of their child's gender identity. You provided them with information about transgender identities and transitions steps, thereby creating a context within which they can understand who their child may be. The conjoint sessions then help the parents understand who their child *is*.

In the conjoint sessions the parents hear from their young person, in detail, about experiences related to gender identity. It is enlightening for parents to hear how their child has experienced gender over time; how they gained certainty (to whatever extent they have so far) about their transgender identity; what distress, if any, they have felt about this so far; and what steps they want to take now and in the future.

For parents who view the child's dysphoria solely as a manifestation of existing or possible mental illness, your concurrent evaluation of any mental health concerns is accompanied by educating the parents about the interactions between transgender identity and mental health. This process helps separate mental health and gender identity considerations. Parents will be reassured if you take clear steps to address any mental health needs.

Sometimes parents have a theory to explain that the transgender identity is not real, but just a reaction to a troubling life circumstance. Generally these circumstances are not the cause of the child's transgender identity. Ehrensaft (2012) has written that it is possible, but rare, for trauma in children to lead to temporary gender confusion. Mock (2014, p.235) states: 'Despite the sacrifices, trans people are still wrongly viewed as being confused. It takes determination and clear, thought-out conviction, not confusion to give up many...privileges to be visibly [oneself].' Often, the youth's awareness of gender difference precedes the trauma in question, while the declaration of trans identity occurred after it. In these instances, a review of the full history clarifies that the transgender identity was not caused by the event. Trauma and loss can have a tremendous impact on a young person's emotional development, independent of gender identity. Address these issues in the trans youth's therapy as you would for any other young person in mental health care.

Many young people on the path to affirming a transgender identity make an effort at some point to embrace their birth-assigned gender more fully, to see if they can will themselves to be cisgender. This can be confusing to parents, who may remark, 'She looked so pretty at the school dance last year. She insisted on getting a new dress for it and having her hair done.' Or, 'Just last year he seemed like such a macho guy, working out all the time and then joining the rugby team.' Mock discusses the same phenomenon, but in her case motivated by pleasing others and getting relief from harassment:

> On the road to self-revelation, we make little compromises in an effort to appease those we love, those who are invested in us, those who have dreams for us. Those people tend to be our parents... I believed I could make [my mother] happy if I were the kid she'd always wanted, the one who stopped all the girlie stuff that had angered my father for years. Mom never asked me to butch up; I just did it, and the world reacted differently... There was no longer a target on my back, and for once it felt good to be invisible, even if I was masked by untruth. (2014, p.98)

A discussion between the youth and the parents about what the youth's intentions and experiences were during this time of strong gender conformance helps parents put these observations in context. For some youth, this experience of trying to meet familial and societal expectations clarifies the false nature of this expression and the truth of their transgender identity.

'Embracing transgender identity will lead to harassment or physical harm'

Most children are living in communities that frown on strongly discordant gender expression. Transgender teens who were gender nonconforming as children may have been bullied by peers or mistreated by adults (Menvielle and Hill 2010; Toomey *et al.* 2010). Parents expect harassment will worsen if their child comes out as transgender. On the other hand, being unable to live authentically can harm the young person's mental health and self-esteem and affect their social functioning (Brill and Pepper 2008; Kuvalanka, Weiner and Mahan 2014). These are the potential consequences when parents do not allow a social transition. The school is responsible for creating a safe environment and parents are responsible for finding a safe and supportive school for their child. The next chapter of this book focuses on advocating at school.

The teens I worked with who made a gender transition at school were accepted by most of their peers, often with what I call 'supportive indifference': a shrug of the shoulders, a low-key supportive comment, and then an effort to use the correct name and pronouns. These teens were students at public and private high schools in Connecticut, in a liberal area of the United States. For most, harassment did not increase when they made a social transition at school. Many of those whose gender nonconformance had previously led to harassment were *more* accepted by peers once they made a transition to their affirmed gender. My impression is that these students seemed more confident after transition and as a result got more positive responses from peers. This was the experience of Katie Rain Hill when she came out as transgender:

> When I was Luke – a feminine, nerdy boy – kids teased me because I was different and because they didn't understand who or what I was. And at the time, I didn't understand who or what I was either. Now, though, I knew who I was…and I was eager to let people get to know me… I learned that when you're up front and confident about yourself, you're often treated with respect. (2014, p.153)

In schools that have addressed diversity and bullying, it is likely that more students are prepared to accept this news with an open mind (Horn and Romeo 2010). Parents who hear about the positive experiences of other students are more optimistic about the responses their youth may receive.

Most teens come out to some of their friends before telling their parents. To this degree they have tested their environment and have a sense that it will be reasonable to proceed. When teens do not feel safe coming out at school, or if things turn out worse than they expected, home schooling or a small alternative school are usually the best options. One of the advantages of parent involvement before the teen makes a transition at school is that parents can advocate in advance with school administration for a protective response when the student comes out.

And what about parents who fear that their child will be physically harmed? Some transgender youth do experience violence (Milrod 2014). On the other hand, blocking the possibility of transition increases the risk of depression, substance abuse and self-harm (Andrews 2014; Hidalgo *et al.* 2013; Lev 2004; Riley *et al.* 2011). These dangers loom when parents refuse a teen's request to transition. The balance of safety and authenticity cannot include delays that the youth finds intolerable.

'Our child will have an unhappy future as a transgender person'

Some parents anticipate a bleak future for their transgender child: no friends, no job and no love relationship. Parents feel more hopeful after hearing about positive outcomes for others. Let them know about the kinds of transgender youth experiences you have witnessed and encourage them to read memoirs and connect with other parents through PFLAG or a local parents' support group. It is also important to point out to them that the alternative, hiding one's authentic gender identity in order to gain access to jobs or relationships, can cause tremendous sadness and distress. You can use the exercise described in Chapter 2 to help them reflect on their own experiences with authenticity and safety. This will help them develop greater empathy for their child's current challenges. On reflection, most parents will see the value in being true to oneself, rather than focusing primarily on how others may react.

Fitting in is a challenge for teens and young adults. For transgender youth the challenge can be especially tough. Young people need their parents' support when they are struggling with authentic expression, integrity and the risk of rejection. This is the case even when some parents at the same time fear disapproval for having a transgender child. If parents can get past their discomfort with transgender identity and unconventional gender expression, they will be able to focus on what their young person needs at this challenging time. With your help, parents will find it is possible to pay attention to authenticity and safety at the same time.

'Our child is too young. When they are older they will regret steps they take now'

Parents may feel that time spent living in the affirmed gender becomes a source of embarrassment if the youth reverses course in the future. They may worry that their teen or even their young adult is acting precipitously in making a social transition, that they are too young to know who they really are. Most adults can think of something they believed about themselves as a teen or young adult that they no longer find to be true. It is important to help parents understand that transgender identity for teens and young adults is generally not something they are just trying out on a whim, and that the social transition is a very useful step in gaining clarity. It is also likely to provide the young person some relief from dysphoria. Worrying about how others may react can get in the way of seeing what is best for the child. Parents understandably feel caught between 'the fear of being too accepting and therefore exposing their child to danger...and the fear of damaging their child's personality by not allowing them full liberty to express themselves' (Malpas 2011, p.466). I try to help the family find ways to create as much safety as possible while allowing the young person full and authentic self-expression.

In Chapter 10 I discussed the rationales for medical transition steps at various ages. Sharing these ideas with parents helps them get a better sense of the pros and cons of allowing their teen to make the medical changes the youth is requesting. Remind parents that you will carry out a full assessment before recommending medical intervention. Parents may fear that you are starting out with the assumption that their child will need to make a gender transition. Assure them that you understand their fears. It is generally helpful to let them know that in some instances the assessment leads to an understanding of gender identity that does not include a need for medical intervention. The goal is to find out what is best for their child. Let parents know that you are initiating this discussion about their child without expecting a particular outcome.

Parents will also benefit from learning what we now know about gender identity persistence and regrets after transition. After the young person shares their history of gender identity awareness and development with the parents, you can highlight the elements of that history that give you confidence about any transition steps you are recommending. Let them know about the research showing gender identity persistence and good psychosocial outcomes for youth who initiate medical transition at age 16 (de Vries *et al.* 2014; Reed *et al.* 2008). Getting to know other families whose teens began medical transition at the same age as their child, and who are doing well a number of years later, is highly reassuring for these parents. Richard Pleak (2009, p.286) reports 'a growing international consensus that once kids [reach age 12 or] 13, gender atypicality or gender variance is not going to change much going forward.' Research by Steensma *et al.* (2011) suggests ages 10–13 as a time of consolidation of a gender identity that will hold as the young person continues through adolescence into adulthood.

'There is no need to transition. People are no longer limited by gender'

Some parents point out to their teen or young adult that, in their view, people are no longer constrained by gender in what they can pursue or accomplish in their lives. If the child is romantically attracted to those of the same birth sex, they point out that cisgender gay and lesbian people live happy lives, as if the young person's motivation for gender transition is simply to be perceived as heterosexual. It does not seem to the parents that gender transition is needed. This includes many open-minded parents who feel that at this time in our culture a girl can do anything a boy can do and vice versa.

I explain to these parents that the fundamental purpose of embracing one's transgender identity is not to gain access to gendered activities, jobs or relationships. Rather, there are three core issues for most transgender people seeking transition: the sex they were assigned at birth is wrong for them; they want others to see them as the gender they feel they are inside; and some (or all) of the gendered aspects of their bodies feel wrong to them. To help parents to grasp this, as it is foreign to their own experience, I identify the elements of their child's narrative that illustrate one or more of these points. These factors may seem more complex and more difficult to understand when the young person's identity is non-binary. Counsel the youth to be patient with their parents. It may take longer than the young person expects for parents to gain a full understanding of these concepts.

'This is happening too fast'
One common scenario is that of the transgender teen who comes out to parents after a long period of thinking about gender, researching on the internet, disclosing to supportive friends and watching videos of other youth who are happily in the process of hormone therapy. The youth tells their parents they are transgender and they want to see a therapist for a referral for hormones. Even if their child was gender nonconforming, even if the parents have wondered if they might grow up to be gay or lesbian, and even if they were perfectly comfortable with that possible outcome, most of these parents have not considered that their child might be transgender. They are surprised by and unprepared for this disclosure. The idea of their child undergoing cross-sex hormone treatment is alien to them and frightening.

Many parents arrived at my office shortly after their child's disclosure with exactly these reactions. After assuring them that we would proceed cautiously to figure out what is best, I shared with them and with the youth my usual time frame for completing an evaluation and considering a referral for hormone therapy. I have listed my time guidelines in Chapter 10 in case you are new to this work and do not have your own sense of how long this may take. It is helpful to let parents know if you are new to this process and may therefore take a little more time to reach a decision. If you have limited experience, I suggest you arrange supervision so you can review your cases with a more knowledgeable clinician. Let the family know you will be doing so. Explain as well that factors such as age, non-binary identities, social detachment or autism spectrum disorders can slow the process down. As the evaluation proceeds, alert both the youth and the parent to any new information that would cause you to recommend taking more time or speeding things up.

The pace of transition steps becomes a negotiation between the youth and the parents, facilitated by the therapist. When counseling the youth to be patient about the need to take things slowly, remind them that they are fortunate to have their parents engaged in treatment and open to discussion. Even if they are over 18, and able to make decisions without their parents' consent, it is worthwhile to wait a bit to gain their parents' support. When advocating with the parents to move more quickly than they had expected, highlight the reversible nature of social transition and puberty blockers. For fully or partially irreversible treatments, explain your reasons for wanting to move more quickly, such as concerns about the youth's irreversible pubertal developments, their level of depression or distress or their risk of self-harm. I have found that if all parties stay engaged in treatment, it is generally possible to arrive at a time frame agreeable to all. Be patient with the process. Often what seems to be an irreconcilable disagreement shifts suddenly when one party is able to understand the other's point of view.

'What did we do wrong?'

Some parents feel at fault for their child's trans identity (Menvielle *et al.* 2005). Parents who refused to get their son the doll he wanted wonder if by suppressing his feminine expression they caused it to build over time into a female identity. Others, who allowed their son to play with dolls and remained neutral about his feminine expression wonder if these actions led him to grow up feeling that he was a girl. Parents of 'tomboys' who supported their daughter's rough and tumble play wonder if they failed to encourage her feminine side enough. Did she somehow intuit that they were disappointed about having three daughters and had wished that one were a boy? Did a single mom fail to provide adult male role models for her son when his father was absent? Parents have various ideas about what caused their child to be transgender. Some of these ideas place the parents front and center.

I tell parents that their actions and attitudes did not cause their child's gender identity. The cause of transgender identity is unknown and presumed to be multifactorial (Diamond 2006; Erickson-Schroth 2013). Marco Hildalgo and his colleagues suggest that the child's gender identity is:

> ...informed by a complex interplay of cultural, social, geographic, and interpersonal factors... Those whose behaviors (and/or dysphoria) 'persist' do so even while vulnerable to facing considerable isolation and disdain from family, peers and others, and often without many media models or others with whom to identify. This suggests a strong constitutional component for gender-nonconforming children, albeit one never exempt from environmental forces. (Hidalgo *et al.* 2013, p.288)

On the other hand, I point out to parents that their behaviors and attitudes do have a strong impact on their children's self-esteem and social comfort (Malpas 2011). I emphasize the importance of loving and accepting their children as they are now. Parents who criticized or shamed their child for gender nonconforming behaviors, thereby diminishing their emotional well-being, can now respond supportively, providing a corrective emotional experience (Crawford 2003). We know that parental support improves the self-esteem and mental health of transgender youth (Travers *et al.* 2012).

Some responses that may seem acceptable to parents are hurtful to the young person. These include asking them to alter their presentation to a more conforming one at family gatherings; suggesting that grandpa will 'have a heart attack' if he learns his grandchild is transgender; refusing to allow LGBT friends to socialize at your house; promoting religious prohibitions on cross-gender expression or suggesting that there will be punishment for those who are LGBT; and suggesting that the child's self-expression is shameful for the family. Parents may view these behaviors as emphasizing safety and not realize how damaging they can be to the child's self-esteem and social development (Ryan 2009; Travers *et al.* 2012).

Here are some positive steps parents can take (adapted from Ryan 2009). These actions may mean much more to a youth than parents imagine:

- Talk with your child about their trans identity with an attitude of curiosity, affection and wanting to help.
- Put aside your own discomfort when interacting with your child. Get help with these feelings elsewhere.
- Do not categorize anyone's hurtful behavior as 'understandable' or something your child should just accept.
- Bring them to LGBT events or trans support groups.
- Attend support groups for parents.
- Speak up about any trans-negative attitudes in your faith community.
- Find trans adults who can be positive role models.

'This is embarrassing'

Some parents are highly uncomfortable about having a transgender teen or young adult. The concept of different gender identities is completely foreign to them. Based on their upbringing and experiences, parents may view transgender people as sick or sinful. They may be disgusted that their child would affiliate with this group. Talk with these parents about the beliefs that underlie their feelings. As Menvielle *et al.* (2005, p.45) say: 'Pointing out that the child is not hurting anyone and that the parents' discomfort comes from conscious or unconscious prejudice can be very important.' Educate them about the variety of gender identities that exist. Some parents may be familiar with transgender identities but unaware of non-binary identities. Emphasize that gender identities exist on a continuum, and transgender identities are among the many variations that naturally occur in human nature.

Ask parents what they value and cherish about their child. Remind them that gender is only one aspect of who their child is. The other qualities they admire will persist. I recommend conducting these discussions initially with the parents alone, so they can speak freely without fear of hurting their child. By validating their initial concerns and then providing new information, you can help parents put aside feelings based on ignorance and prejudice. It is easier then to focus on the important questions of authenticity and safety for their young person. I have seen parents move from being ashamed and angry to becoming advocates for their child and celebrating their uniqueness.

Many parents worry about how others will react to the news that their child is transgender. This may include friends, neighbors, co-workers, family members and the parents of their child's friends and peers. It is helpful to validate these feelings as common to many parents, but keep the focus on how the parents can support their child and make decisions that are in the youth's best interest. Some parents 'experience secondary stigmatization that can result in isolation and feelings of shame' (Menvielle and Tuerk 2002, p.1010). Encourage these parents to decrease their isolation by sharing their feelings with supportive adults. These may be family members and friends who they know are open-minded, or other parents of transgender youth.

Parents who are deeply ashamed will need extra help. It may even be difficult for them to remain in treatment. Do your best to stay connected to these parents, whose shame often manifests as anger toward their child, a supportive co-parent or the therapist. It may not be possible for them to examine and challenge the transphobic assumptions that underlie their shame. They may find any suggestion to do so to be 'unrealistic' and ignorant of others' hostility toward and disapproval of trans people. Keep in mind that these parents may be fundamentally motivated by fears for their child's safety, although they are also motivated to protect their standing in the eyes of others. As Ryan (2010, p.13) has written: 'Families want the best for their children – even if the way they express their care and concern is experienced as rejection by their LBGT children.'

The approach I have found most helpful with parents who express shame is to ask them to choose one person who is likely to respond negatively and share the information with them. The goal is to externalize the shame, to move it from self-condemnation based on others' anticipated responses to experiencing an actual negative response. The actual response is often much less negative than expected. But if there is a harshly critical or condemning response, it is likely to elicit the parent's protective instincts for the child they love, and motivate them to take their child's side.

Parents who are viscerally angry and highly ashamed can try this out as an exercise instead: they can imagine or role play the negative encounter, see what that stirs up in them, and try out a response on their part that defends their child, even if they do not fully endorse the child's trans identity themselves. Unfortunately, some of the parents who were most angry dropped out of treatment, often before there was an opportunity to address their shame and anger. So the first goal with these angry parents is to keep them connected to treatment, for the child's sake. In some instances when a parent dropped out, the child was also, sadly, pulled from treatment. For some, another parent remained engaged in treatment with the child and carried out the negotiations with the angry parent when the time came to consider transition steps.

One final consideration on the topic of embarrassment is the understandable concern that many parents have for the siblings of a youth who transitions. While I have found that this process generally does not cause dismay or confusion for significantly older or younger sibs, some who are within a year or two in age encounter social challenges or worry about peer responses to their sibling transitioning. I often include the siblings close in age once it seems clear that the youth is moving toward a social transition. What I have found is that many of the siblings are unconcerned. They expect their friends to be accepting and do not anticipate trouble from other peers.

There have been a few who were worried about how their friends would react or how their sibling's transition could affect the way their peers view them. In the family sessions we arrived at an adjustment to the youth's social transition plan, so the sibling would have a little more time or perhaps an upcoming school break to speak to friends and establish supports in advance of their sibling coming out. In all instances things went smoothly, and the transitioning youth understood the need to wait a bit longer for the official transition at school. I expect that this challenge will be more difficult for families in other areas of the country and the world where the support I found so common among middle and high school students in Connecticut is not as likely to be prevalent. Each family's situation needs to be addressed individually, as the relevant details will vary greatly. I would not expect the parents to have to sacrifice the needs of one child for another, but rather to be able to negotiate a plan that is manageable for all and respectful of the needs of all of the siblings involved.

'This is a loss for us'

When a child strongly affirms a transgender identity, many parents experience a deep feeling of loss. Parent–child relationships incorporate societal notions of what it means to be a parent of a certain gender with a child of the same or a different gender. When parents find out their child will be changing to conform to a long-felt but previously secret gender identity, it may seem as if the young person they know is being replaced by a stranger. Jane Baker wrote this about her experience with her 20-year-old child:

> The disappearance of my son – even though he was replaced by my daughter – felt like a death… I grieved the loss of my former child. Of course, Steven was not truly dead, but he ceased to exist as I'd known him his entire life. (Baker 2015, p.45)

It helps parents to know that these feelings are common (Menvielle *et al.* 2005; Vanderburgh 2009). Parents may need to grieve. In a spirit of open communication, some parents mention these feelings of loss to their child. This can be appropriate if done sensitively, but it is not helpful to burden the child further with the parent's grief. Parents can turn to other adults for that support. Young people will generally assure their parents that from their point of view they are simply becoming more congruent with who they really are. They are fundamentally the same person they were before. This is easier for parents to see if their child had been somewhat gender nonconforming all along. A number of the parents I worked with went back to look at childhood photos and could see that their child's inherent femininity or masculinity was always visible. They just never viewed it as an indication of a different gender identity.

One of the best remedies for parents' sadness is seeing their child flourish in their affirmed identity. Many parents have commented to me that they are pleased to have a happy child in the newly affirmed gender after being so worried about the sullen or depressed child they had before. After a 'frenetic inquiry' to gather information about transgender identity, discussions with her child, and witnessing the youth's transformation to female, Baker realized:

> If 'she' was going to emerge as a happy and fulfilled person, then was this quite possibly a cure for his [earlier in life] puzzling

loneliness?... My earlier misconceptions were replaced with a new understanding of my child's gender dissonance and the deep discomfort it had caused. Instead of persuading Steven to change his mind, I became convinced that the transition needed to happen. (Baker 2015, p.45)

ONGOING SUPPORT

This chapter describes what is likely to take place in the first three to six months of family therapy for a transgender youth. Once these tasks are completed, therapy continues on an as-needed or as-wanted basis. This varies greatly from family to family. Generally it means a decrease in the frequency of sessions. Often the structure includes individual sessions, with a parent joining toward the end to share information or discuss any family concerns. In the absence of any mental health concerns or major life stressors accompanying transition steps, there may be significant gaps in treatment. It is important to follow up at least three months after any medical transition step to monitor the youth's adjustment and any need for additional counseling.

In my practice, many of the teens had a prior therapist who initially referred them to me for gender identity evaluation and family consultation. Most of these youth continued to meet with their prior therapist on a regular basis during and after my work with them, only returning to me for intermittent consultation specific to gender identity and transition steps. As with so much of the work with transgender youth, it is important to decide how to proceed case by case for the best outcome for the youth and the family.

FOR FURTHER EXPLORATION

Books

Helping Your Transgender Teen: A Guide for Parents, by Irwin Krieger, Genderwise Press, 2011.

Now What? A Handbook for Families with Transgender Children, by Rex Butt, Transgress Press, 2015.

Trading Places: When Our Son Became a Daughter – A Mother's Story of a Family's Transition, by Jane Baker, Braefield Press, 2014.

The Transgender Teen: A Handbook for Parents and Professsionals Supporting Transgender and Non-Binary Teens, by Stephanie Brill and Lisa Kenney, Cleis Press, 2016.

Transitions of the Heart: Stories of Love, Struggle and Acceptance by Mothers of Transgender and Gender Variant Children, Rachel Pepper, Cleis Press, 2012.

Other written materials

A La Familia, a Spanish/English Guide for families about the Bible, sexuality and gender identity. Available at www.thetaskforce.org/downloads/release_materials/tf_a_la_familia.pdf

Coming Out as Transgender to Your Latino Family; Tips from a Trans Latina Counselor. Available at www.latina.com/lifestyle/our-issues/coming-out-transgender-your-latino-family-tips-trans-latina-counselor

Supportive Families, Healthy Children and a Practitioner's Resource Guide: Helping Families to Support Their LGBT Children. Available at the Family Acceptance Project website: http://familyproject.sfsu.edu. Click on 'Publications.'

Videos

'Becoming Me,' episode 2107 of *In the Life*. Search for this title at www.cinema.ucla.edu

Jacob's Journey: Raising a Transgender Child. Search for this title at www.nbcnews.com

CHAPTER 12

School and Beyond

For teenagers, school is the locus of their 'real-world' experience. Adolescence through young adulthood is a time of identity exploration. It is a time to try out different interests, different friends and different ways of interacting with others. There is an urge to find an authentic self and others who are similar. At the same time there are pressures to fit in with the peer group with the highest status, even if the teen does not share the group's priorities and values. This is a dilemma for most youth, and it is heightened for those who are transgender or gender nonconforming. Self-affirmation will be more difficult if their community of peers maintains rigid ideas about gender. A community with flexible attitudes provides an easier context for gender identity exploration.

MIDDLE AND HIGH SCHOOL

School-based support is essential for middle and high school students who are transgender or exploring variant gender identity and expression. When community attitudes are trans-negative, support at school may not be easy to attain. Positive school support includes the values of understanding, respect, privacy and safety. These are things we all can endorse, regardless of our political and moral views. The components include:

- trusting the student's ability to know who they are
- respecting the student's requests regarding name, pronouns and other gendered language
- honoring a student's privacy
- including the student within their affirmed gender group
- providing comprehensive support and safety for all students.

Trusting the student's ability to know who they are

Sorting out one's gender identity generally happens outside of school. Teens and young adults usually begin with an initial awareness that something is different, then see or hear something about transgender identity that piques their interest, and explore this further with online searches and discussion with close friends. At some point in this process they may tell their parents, or their therapist if they are already in therapy for other issues. By the time the issue is raised formally at school, they also may have conferred with a therapist who specializes in gender identity. It is not the job of school personnel to make a judgment about the veracity of the teen's transgender identity. It is essential to take the teen's declaration of transgender identity at face value and go from there. It is also important to remember that the social transition at school is a fully reversible step and one that helps the teen clarify their understanding of their transgender identity.

Respecting the student's requests regarding name, pronouns and other gendered language

Mental health clinicians can play a vital role in supporting students and parents as they advocate for fair and respectful treatment at school. An important part of the social transition is the use of a student's affirmed name, pronouns and other gendered language such as girl/boy/student ('student' being an example of a gender-neutral word choice). The best practice in this regard, and the one that is mandated in states that have transgender civil rights legislation or trans-supportive educational guidelines, is to use the student's affirmed name and gender marker on all school documents including rosters, exams, report cards and diplomas (McGuire and Conover-Williams 2010). The one exception I am aware of at this time in the United States is in national documentation such as the SAT college admissions exam and the Free Application for Federal Student Aid (FAFSA – required for students applying for financial aid for college). At this time, students can only have their legal name on these documents and must use the gender marker that is listed with the Social Security Administration.

Australia has established a marker for those who identify as neither male nor female (Australian Government 2013). As there are no state or national indicators for non-binary gender identity available in the United States at this time, those who identify as non-binary generally keep their birth-assigned gender marker and only change their name and pronouns. Students' requests for the use of 'they/them/their' or other non-binary pronoun sets may be resisted by peers and adults who find the usage cumbersome or complain that it is not grammatically correct. The youth and supportive adults can explain why these pronouns are important, emphasizing respect for the individual even when this takes practice or sounds wrong to others. In English these pronouns are mostly used when the individual is not present, so it falls on supportive peers and adults to model correct pronoun use and encourage others to do so. Languages that have gender embedded more broadly provide additional challenges for non-binary young people.

A student who is transitioning at a school where they are already known by their former name and gender usually starts by notifying close friends and the school administration in private. If this experience is new for the school, you can help by speaking directly to a school counselor or administrator, with the youth's and the family's permission. Explain the need for the social transition and your recommendations for supportive school responses. Offer to meet with them to discuss the matter further if they are unwilling or feel unable to provide the requested support.

The student then chooses a day to begin going by their new name and pronouns. Teachers will be informed in advance to use the new name and pronouns as of that date. Rosters will be changed so substitute teachers do not call out the old name. Other students generally are not informed directly. They see the changes in the student's presentation and hear the forms of address used by teachers and close friends and either understand and follow suit or ask about it and learn that way. Respectful questions are welcomed. Instances of hostile questioning or insistence on using the old name and pronouns should be viewed by the school as harassment and an indicator that individual students or the student body as a whole need diversity training in this area.

Some schools provide diversity training proactively in advance of a student transitioning. In that case, the teachers are informed that a student will be transitioning but the student group receives the training at a school assembly and is not told it is in relation to a specific student. At the elementary level it may be useful to send a letter home to parents explaining that an unnamed student is transitioning, and offering respectful answers parents can give if their own child has questions about this. See the family and school resources listed in Appendix B for ideas.

Administrators are often worried there will be complaints from other parents who are upset to know that their child is in a class with a student undergoing gender transition. Administrators may also be pressured by the school board or community members to not accommodate the trans student's needs. It is easier for administrators to respond to parents or others who object when state guidelines are in place mandating support for transgender students. But with or without a legal mandate, administrators should emphasize the values of understanding, respect, privacy and safety for all students that underlie how they are handling this child's gender transition at school.

Administrators may also worry that one child's transition will upset or confuse other students. One eighth grade student I worked with thought of herself consistently as a girl and felt uncomfortable continuing to go to school as a boy. This discomfort interfered with her ability to do her best at school. School staff suggested she disclose her female identity to her close friends only. They were worried that if she transitioned at school it would be confusing for the younger students. Since she would be graduating from this school in a few months, they did not think it would be a problem to ask her to wait.

The principal invited me to a meeting to discuss how they would proceed. My role was to address the staff's concerns about the impact on the younger kids, and advocate for this student's right to be authentic and have the best emotional and educational outcome. The plan we came up with, which met everyone's needs, was for the school to arrange a diversity workshop for students in advance of the social transition. There would also be training for teachers about how to understand this student's gender identity and respond to any questions or concerns raised by her peers or by younger students. With this excellent preparation, the school transition took place smoothly. As it turned out, there were few reactions from other students.

Honoring a student's privacy

Even in the absence of transgender civil rights legislation, US students' privacy is protected by the Family Educational Rights and Privacy Act (FERPA) (Paakkonen 2012). This federal law protects the privacy of student education records. Thus, students who arrive at a new school having already transitioned to their affirmed gender have the right to have that information kept private. Generally the student and parents will notify the school principal and school nurse so that any medical emergencies can be handled appropriately. There is no need for peers and teachers and other school staff to know that a teenaged student was assigned a different sex at birth. Again, if this is new for the school, you can assist by meeting with the principal to help them understand your student's needs.

Privacy is also a major concern for students who feel unsafe coming out as transgender to their parents but would like to do so at school. The student may choose to present in their affirmed gender at school while maintaining their birth assigned gender at home.

A social transition at school can provide some of the same benefits as a full social transition. Schools can provide these students a crucial opportunity to live at least part time in their affirmed gender. In this instance the student would speak directly to an administrator or counselor about their need to live authentically at school while feeling unsafe to do so at home. It is challenging for school staff to use affirmed names and pronouns at school and switch to birth name and pronouns when interacting with parents. But schools have accomplished this when it was needed to support the student's authenticity and safety.

In these instances it is important for a school counselor to help the student explore their identity and safety concerns and, if needed, refer them to an outside therapist who is knowledgeable about gender identity. The student can ask their parents to bring them to a therapist without having to disclose the specific focus of treatment. It should suffice to say that the youth is depressed or anxious and not specify exactly what it is about.

Including the student within their affirmed gender group

In non-residential middle and high schools there are only a few gender-segregated activities and facilities. When a transgender student transitions at school or arrives after having transitioned, it is inevitable that concerns will be raised about bathrooms and locker rooms and, for student-athletes, team sports.

The approach that honors a trans student's authenticity, safety and best educational experience is to offer both group and individual bathrooms and changing areas to all students. Transgender students generally want to use either a single bathroom or the group bathroom of their affirmed gender. Some transgender students prefer at first to have access to a private bathroom, particularly if they are transitioning at a school where they are already known in their birth-assigned gender. Administrators are usually most comfortable with this outcome, as they are otherwise likely to face some comments from other students or from the parents of other students. Those who object to a trans female student using the group bathroom may claim there is now 'a boy in the girls' room.' They imagine that the presence of the trans girl somehow puts the cisgender girls at risk.

The approach that honors the rights of all students is to offer the trans student both options. As Janet Mock says:

> When trans students are told they cannot use public facilities, it doesn't only block them from the toilet... It tells them with every sneer, every closed door, that we do not want to see them, that they should go hide and that ultimately they do not belong. (Mock 2017, p.10SR)

If the transgender student's use of a group bathroom causes discomfort to another student, that student should have the option to use a private bathroom for their comfort. There are many reasons a student may want to use a private bathroom, including anxiety relieving themselves in the presence of others, and medical or disability concerns. Discussions about bathroom use are private and confidential to each student, and not to be disclosed to any other student or their parents.

In states with clear transgender rights legislation and school guidelines it may be easier for administrators to assert these policies. In other states, FERPA provides a basis for maintaining privacy. In any case, providing the most respectful consideration for a transgender student is part of providing the best educational experience for all students, which should be every school's mandate.

Locker room use should be handled in the same manner. For students whose transgender identity is private, there should be no concerns raised by other students and their families, as long as the student's privacy is maintained. A student's choice of bathroom and locker room, as well as the extent to which they choose to share knowledge of their trans identity with others, can change over the course of a student's time at a school. This may necessitate renegotiation of these practices, keeping the same principles in mind.

I endorse the view that the purpose of team sports at the middle and high school level is primarily educational and secondarily competitive. Pat Griffin writes:

> An April 2014 letter from the Federal Office of Civil Rights clarified that discrimination against transgender students in schools is covered by Title IX[1] and educators in schools across the United States are accountable for ensuring the safety and inclusion of transgender students in all school-sponsored activities. Athletics is an integral part of the extracurricular program offered in practically every high school in the United States and schools are accountable for ensuring that all students have equal access to participation. Participation in high school sports is recognized as an important aspect of developing positive self-esteem and a connection to school and community as well as a deterrent to the use of alcohol, drugs, tobacco or other unhealthy activities. Ensuring that all students, including transgender students, have the opportunity to participate in a wide variety of school sports experiences complements the academic mission of schools...
>
> Concern about maintaining 'competitive equity' is one of the most often expressed reservations about transgender girls competing on girls teams. As with concerns about safety, several assumptions are embedded in this concern: That transgender girls are always more skilled, stronger and bigger than their non-transgender teammates and opponents. There is no research to support the contention that enabling a transgender girl to play on a girls team creates a competitive imbalance. In reality, the overlap in skill and performance in sports among biological males and females and the wide variance within each gender group are important considerations to remember in addressing concerns about competitive equity. (Griffin 2015)

---

1   Title IX is a law passed in 1972 that requires gender equity for boys and girls in every educational program that receives US government funding.

Asserting this viewpoint can be a major challenge when the school climate is unwelcoming. Many trans youth feel their only option is to take a break from participation in sports. Hopefully this situation will improve as legal protections advance and more students come out as transgender.

Residential middle and high schools, as well as residential mental health treatment facilities, have the additional challenge of placing transgender students in gender-segregated housing. I am not aware of any policies that have been drafted to guide residential schools and facilities regarding housing transgender students. Based on what many colleges offer incoming transgender students, it seems that the best option, if it is available, is a single bedroom in the housing for students of the trans student's affirmed gender. Thus a trans boy would have a single in the boys' house, dorm or hospital wing. When no single rooms are available, my recommendation is that the staff speak with the student's more open-minded peers and their parents, to the extent that the trans student and their family allow, to find a housing combination that is comfortable and affirming for the trans student and the peers who will be sharing space with them. While many colleges now have gender-neutral dorms, that is unlikely to be the case in residential high schools and middle schools.

Providing comprehensive support and safety for all students
Safety is a significant concern for transgender students and their families. GLSEN's 2015 National (US) School Climate Survey found that the majority of LGBTQ students felt unsafe at school and experienced verbal and sexual harassment. Many had experienced physical assault and cyberbullying. The majority of those who were harassed or assaulted did not inform school staff, because they did not expect to get a helpful response. Those who did report found that most often they did not receive a helpful response. Many were told to just ignore the aggression against them. More than half of the LGBTQ students had overheard insulting remarks about LGBTQ people from teachers or other school staff. For the majority

of transgender students, the school did not honor their affirmed name and pronouns and required them to use the bathroom corresponding to their legal sex (GLSEN 2016).

The survey goes on to show that these negative effects were mitigated by the presence of gay–straight alliances (GSAs), LGBT-inclusive curricula, supportive educators and comprehensive bullying and harassment policies. Regionally in the United States, students in the Northeast and the West reported lower levels of negative language and victimization related to sexual orientation and gender expression than students in the South and the Midwest. LGBT-related resources were most available in the Northeast. Students in rural and small towns reported the highest frequency of anti-LGBT language and discrimination, and the lowest likelihood of having LGBT-related school resources and supports.

Schools and the parent community need to hear from LGBT students, their parents and LGBT adults in the community (including school staff members if they feel safe to come out) about their experiences. The progress of the LGBT civil rights movement demonstrates that people are more receptive to supporting diversity in gender and sexual orientation when they personally know someone who is LGBT. The first parent in a given school who advocates for their transgender child at school will be paving the way for the next parent at that school. Parents can link their efforts to the school's anti-bullying program if one is in place, or join with other parents to urge the school to establish a program. You may be able to assist by providing information or facilitating discussions that enhance the family's effort to create a more welcoming school.

Jeff Perrotti (2014) recommends that school administrators who want to do their best for transgender students can:

- reach out for information from the LGBT community and local experts in LGBT rights and mental health
- designate one or more school staff to coordinate efforts on behalf of transgender students

- view the process as a collaboration between parents and school
- provide inservice training for staff and assemblies for students covering diversity, including but not limited to gender diversity
- establish and maintain an active anti-bullying/harassment program, with an expectation of adult intervention to stop harassment
- maintain strict confidentiality about any student's LGBT status that they have not shared openly
- confer with other school administrators who have successfully supported a transgender student
- plan at-school transition and support steps for each transgender student
- designate time for staff to talk with each transgender student about their challenges and progress.

DATING AND SEX

Dating is not simple for anyone at any age, but for transgender youth it is simplest when they meet someone within a social context where they are known to be transgender. If the couple explores physical intimacy, it is easier for the trans youth to be explicit about what touch they find comfortable and respectful of their gender identity. If they are also out to their partner's peers and family, the youth and their partner do not have to expend energy on maintaining secrecy from people close to them.

When trans youth consider dating people who do not already know they are transgender, the choices are complicated. For a young trans woman dating a cisgender male who does not know she is transgender, there is a significant risk of violence if she eventually discloses or if he finds out from someone else that she is transgender. The partner may fear that he will be viewed by others as gay, and may feel deeply ashamed about that. He may strike out in anger and shame, or to validate his masculinity in the eyes of others.

While the most authentic and safe approach to dating for trans youth of all genders would seem to be to disclose transgender identity early, this creates other risks. If disclosing early leads to rejection by a potential partner who is not well known to the youth, there is a significant risk that this person will share the youth's private information with others. This constitutes a damaging loss of privacy and creates an increased risk of harassment. Many trans individuals try to find a middle ground of getting to know someone slowly and only disclosing if they are very interested and the partner seems safe. Then it becomes worth taking the risk. If not, they end the dating relationship without ever having come out to this person.

Trans youth are also at risk of remaining in a relationship in which they are validated in their affirmed gender but mistreated in other ways. Being viewed as desirable and attractive in one's affirmed gender is a powerful motivator to stay in a problematic relationship. As a therapist your role is to help your clients understand these dynamics and find a reasonable balance between their need for validation and the importance of staying physically and emotionally safe.

De Vries *et al.* discuss attitudes toward dating and sex among transgender youth and the value of counseling:

A 13-year-old interested in dating but not genital sexual touching or penetration will likely experience less discomfort relating to genital incongruence (or will find it easier to suppress the discomfort) than an 18-year-old who is more interested in pursuing sexual relationships. It has been our experience that quite a few adolescents with GID[2] entirely refrain from dating and sexual activity. The adolescent may feel uncertain because they are afraid to tell the partner about their gender identity problem (if they still live in the original gender role) or about their biological sex (if they have already made the role change).

---

2   GID (Gender Identity Disorder) was the mental health diagnosis in use at the time this article was written.

If reluctance to disclose transgender identity to a partner only seems to be a matter of communication skill, it may be helpful to discuss pros and cons of various options, and to role-play or rehearse explanations to imaginary partners. There is no single 'right moment' or 'right way' for disclosure, but the better prepared and the more confident an adolescent is, the easier it will be to overcome the barriers. (de Vries *et al.* 2006, pp.88–9)

Important elements of sexual safety for trans youth include being able to talk about sexual interests, set limits on sexual interactions, clarify consent, and practice safer sex (Keo-Meier and Hicks 2014). Schools vary widely in the extent to which they include attention to LGBT concerns in sex education classes. According to the National Clearinghouse on Families and Youth, some states in the United States:

...have laws known as 'no promo homo' laws that prohibit educators in public schools from discussing lesbian, gay, bisexual, transgender, and questioning (LGBTQ) people, issues or history, or only allow discussion in a negative light... [Others] have robust transgender health services embedded in their state or local health departments. Additionally, nine states, including Oregon and California, have mandates that require inclusive discussion of sexual orientation and identity in sex education programs. (National Clearinghouse on Families and Youth 2016c)

Additional advocacy is needed to improve education policies and ensure that these policies are carried out by schools.

You can provide an opportunity in therapy for a young person to sort out sexual feelings and consider ways to express them to a partner. The Human Rights Campaign's 'Safer Sex for Trans Bodies' is a good resource for discussing these matters with a teen client. (See listings at the end of this chapter.) You can also be a sounding board to help a young person weigh the excitement of a new relationship and the validation that comes with it against any signs of potential danger.

SUPPORTIVE AND HOSTILE ENVIRONMENTS

Most of the young people I have worked with had a relatively supportive response to their social transition at school. For some, the nature of the support from girls and boys differed. One student commented after disclosing his FTM transition to peers, 'The girls want to talk all about it, ask questions and tell you how supportive they are. The guys just take the information in and are on to the next thing.' Sometimes trans kids are quick to find cisgender peers of their affirmed gender who include them in gender-segregated social groupings. This is tremendously affirming when it happens. Sometimes that takes a while.

The US Departments of Justice and Education issued guidance in May of 2016 indicating that schools may not discriminate against transgender students. The Department of Justice press release states:

> The guidance explains that when students or their parents, as appropriate, notify a school that a student is transgender, the school must treat the student consistent with the student's gender identity. A school may not require transgender students to have a medical diagnosis, undergo any medical treatment, or produce a birth certificate or other identification document before treating them consistent with their gender identity.
>
> The guidance also explains schools' obligations to:
>
> - Respond promptly and effectively to sex-based harassment of all students, including harassment based on a student's actual or perceived gender identity, transgender status or gender transition;
> - Treat students consistent with their gender identity even if their school records or identification documents indicate a different sex;
> - Allow students to participate in sex-segregated activities and access sex-segregated facilities consistent with their gender identity; and

- Protect students' privacy related to their transgender status under Title IX and the Family Educational Rights and Privacy Act.

(US Department of Justice 2016)

There is no guarantee that a school district will heed the instructions in the guidance, even though it is based on law. Many trans youth and their families have to fight for fair treatment. Often legal help is needed. See Appendix B for legal groups and transgender advocacy groups that can help families get fair treatment for their student.

What about youth who do not feel a social transition is possible at their school because it is such a hostile environment? While it is essential to work toward making all schools safe and welcoming, for a youth who is ready to explore gender identity but is in a hostile environment, changing to a safer school may be necessary (Milrod 2014). A number of my teen clients have transferred to smaller, alternative schools in their community. Once settled in there, they felt safe transitioning to their affirmed gender. These transitions have gone smoothly. Most of their new peers were supportive. Parents and child were relieved that there was an opportunity to try out the affirmed gender identity in a safe setting, as a step toward greater certainty about gender identity and possible irreversible transition steps.

COLLEGE

For high school seniors who are going on to college and are already aware of their transgender identity, there are advantages to having their gender transition well underway by the time they graduate from high school. If they have gained certainty about their transgender identity by the fall of their senior year of high school, they can look for colleges that are known to be trans-friendly and disclose their transgender identity in their application. Since trans-friendly schools are generally those that value diversity, acknowledgment of transgender identity on an application can be a plus. Even those who are planning to keep their trans identity private are likely to find the atmosphere at a trans-friendly school more in accord with their values.

All colleges should have clear diversity and anti-bullying policies that are communicated to all students on admission and reinforced as needed. Transgender students who are going away to college, rather than commuting from home, can make housing requests in accordance with their gender identity. Making changes to documentation such as driver license, passport and social security listing may be easier from home rather than while away at school. Prior documentation changes also make the college enrollment process simpler.

Housing for incoming transgender students is easiest at schools that provide gender-neutral housing. In other schools, the most common arrangement is to provide a private room for incoming transgender students in a dorm or wing that houses students of their affirmed gender identity. Schools that do not offer singles for first-year students and have no gender-neutral housing have to handle this challenge sensitively on a case-by-case basis.

For students who were not able to come out as trans in high school because of a lack of support and safety, attending a socially liberal college can be wonderfully affirming. These students and those who first affirm their transgender identity once they are already in college will have the option of transitioning while there. Students who transition at college are usually residing with students of their birth-assigned gender. The students I have worked with who made a gender transition and planned to continue living in gender-segregated dorms were able to arrange for a single or find a group of peers of their affirmed gender to share living space the following year. Off-campus housing is another option for students at some schools. Parents and other adults are often surprised to see how open-minded and accepting many college-age youth are about a peer's gender identity. Many are not troubled at all about having a transgender roommate, nor do they feel that it somehow stigmatizes them. Rather, they may feel that living with others who are different is a valuable part of a college education. If a student has chosen a trans-friendly campus to begin with, all of this will be easier.

Colleges in the United States are guided by the National Collegiate Athletic Association (NCAA), which has established a policy to address the participation of transgender students in college team sports:

> The benefits of school sports participation include many positive effects on physical, social, and emotional well-being. All students, including those who are transgender, deserve access to these benefits. When athletics departments adopt inclusive policies, they are living up to the educational values of equality that join them with the broad institutional and societal ideal of inclusion and respect for differences. (NCAA Office of Inclusion 2011)

Specifically, the NCAA policy states that a trans male student who is being treated with testosterone can compete only on a men's team. A trans female student can compete on a women's team after she has completed one year of testosterone suppression treatment.

ESTABLISHING INDEPENDENCE

A young adult needs employment to become self-sufficient. Workplace protections for transgender employees vary by location and by employer. When non-discrimination laws or company policies are in place, the workplace environment for transgender people can be welcoming. The workplace climate may be better or worse than local laws and company intentions would suggest, as attitudes of co-workers also vary according to their own political, religious and personal beliefs.

According to the 2015 US Transgender Survey, about a quarter of the respondents who were working or looking for work reported losing a job, not getting a promotion or not being hired because of their gender identity or expression. A larger percentage reported mistreatment ranging from harassment based on gender expression to physical and sexual assault. A majority of the respondents who were working reported hiding or delaying their transition or quitting their job to avoid harassment (National Center for Transgender Equality 2016).

As these statistics show, gaining and keeping employment as well as one's experiences at work are all affected by the climate in the workplace. A need to be secretive creates stress, distance from co-workers and difficulty participating in job-related social events. Worries about harassment or job retention can lead to distraction, difficulty concentrating and poor performance. Many companies institute non-discrimination policies so they can hire from the largest applicant pool and have more productive employees.

It is difficult to make general suggestions about job seeking and workplace transition for transgender youth, as the circumstances vary greatly based on location, employer and the attitudes of managers and co-workers. Concerns about keeping one's transgender identity private while applying, as well as while on the job, also vary tremendously. What I have found most helpful in counseling transgender youth about seeking work or coming out on the job is to examine both authenticity and safety concerns. The legal organizations listed in Appendix B provide assistance for those facing workplace discrimination. They can also answer questions about the rights of job applicants and employees.

Over my years of practice I have seen a number of young adults who were stalled after high school or after completing a year or two of college. Their progress regarding school and work was at a standstill. They were living at home with their parents. They tended to have limited local social contacts; they were in touch with friends elsewhere by phone or online. As a result, they spent most of their time in the house. They were inconsistent in their intentions for additional schooling, and extremely slow in applying for jobs. Given the sluggish job market at that time, it was not possible to gain employment with only very occasional job applications. Their approach to gender transition was hesitant as well. They affirmed a clear and consistent sense of transgender identity with a persistent intention to transition, but they did not take any steps in that direction other than informing friends and participating in psychotherapy.

For these young adults, the lack of energy in their gender transition was a manifestation of a general lack of initiative rather than uncertainty about gender. Progress in therapy was slow but over time each of these individuals took some steps to progress with school, work, social life or gender transition. I offered encouragement when they were self-critical and helped them identify small attainable steps they could pursue. They expressed some sadness about being stuck, and some fears about how their transition would go, but maintained optimism about a happy future in their affirmed gender. Some were evaluated for antidepressants, but none received significant benefit from psychiatric medication. Their condition seemed to be one of temperament rather than mood.

Fortunately, some of their goals were synergistic. For example, getting a driver's license could lead to more employment options; getting a job would create more financial wherewithal to begin transition steps. I was struck by their patience with slow progress, when so many of my young clients were in a rush to start medical intervention. I found that being supportive and equally patient was the most helpful stance on my part.

One of the demands of working with transgender youth is the need to rethink your assumptions about how various aspects of young people's lives may unfold. You will find that gender identity exploration and transition add complexities that are not evident at first. In Chapter 13 I will offer my thoughts about how this work will present you with new challenges and expand your horizons.

FOR FURTHER EXPLORATION

Books and articles

Becoming Nicole: The Transformation of an American Family, by Amy Ellis Nutt, Random House, 2015.

'Creating spaces to support transgender youth,' by McGuire and Conover-Williams, *The Prevention Researcher 17*, 4, 17–20, 2010.

'Employment,' by Stirba, Goldstein and Gentili with Reynolds, Hill-Meyer and Scarborough, in *Trans Bodies, Trans Selves* (edited by Laura Erickson-Schroth), Oxford University Press, 2014.

Trans-supportive educational guidelines from US states and federal government
MASSACHUSETTS:

Guidance for Massachusetts Public Schools Creating a Safe and Supportive School Environment: Nondiscrimination on the Basis of Gender Identity, published by the Massachusetts Department of Elementary and Secondary Education, February 2013. Available at www.doe.mass.edu/sfs/lgbtq/GenderIdentity.docx

NEW YORK:

Guidance to School Districts for Creating a Safe and Supportive School Environment for Transgender and Gender Nonconforming Students, published by The State Education Department/The University of the State of New York, July 2015. Available at www.p12.nysed.gov/dignityact/documents/Transg_GNCGuidanceFINAL.pdf

WASHINGTON STATE:

'Prohibiting Discrimination in Washington Public Schools,' in *Guidelines for School Districts to Implement,* produced by the Office of Superintendent of Public Instruction, February 2012. Available at www.k12.wa.us/Equity/pubdocs/ProhibitingDiscriminationInPublicSchools.pdf

US DEPARTMENTS OF JUSTICE AND
EDUCATION JOINT GUIDANCE:

'Dear Colleague' Letter on Transgender Students. Available at www2.ed.gov/about/offices/list/ocr/letters/colleague-201605-title-ix-transgender.pdf; or go to www.ed.gov and search for 'transgender guidance.'

Online resources
Campus Pride has information on LGBTQ-friendly colleges at: www.campusprideindex.org

Gender Spectrum: *Schools in Transition: A Guide for Supporting Transgender Students in K-12 Schools.* Available at www.genderspectrum.org/studenttransitions

GLSEN: search for these at www.glsen.org:
- 'Model District Policy on Transgender and Gender Nonconforming Students'
- 'Safe Space Kit'
- Resources for educators including: 'Educator Guides,' 'LGBT-Inclusive Curriculum' and 'Lesson Plans on Bullying, Bias, and Diversity.'

GSA Network has resources for developing a GSA. Available at www.gsanetwork.org

Human Rights Campaign: *Safer Sex for Trans Bodies*. Available at www.hrc.org/resources/safer-sex-for-trans-bodies

Lambda Legal: search for these at www.lambdalegal.org:
- *Bending the Mold: An Action Kit for Transgender Students.*
- 'Know Your Rights' factsheet for transgender college students.

On the Team: Equal Opportunities for Transgender Student Athletes, by Dr. Pat Griffin and Helen J. Carroll. Available at: www.wiaa.com/ConDocs/Con550/TransgenderStudentAthleteReport.pdf

Trans Student Educational Resources: *Comprehensive Model Policy on Transgender Students*. Available at: www.transstudent.org/modelfouryearpolicy.pdf

Trans Youth Equality Foundation: *College 101: A Guide to Navigating College.* Available at www.transyouthequality.org/college-101

Tyler Clementi Foundation has anti-bullying resources at: http://tylerclementi.org/resources

Video

GLAD: Search for 'Got LGBTQ Rights? Yes!' on youtube.com

CHAPTER 13

Looking Forward

What can you expect as you expand your clinical work to include transgender teens and young adults and their families? Expect to arrive at a new understanding of gender as an aspect of identity that exists on a spectrum and is not always congruent with sexual anatomy. You will learn to see who a person is inside even when their exterior seems to suggest they are someone else. You will be amazed by the many different combinations of gender identities, ways of expression and sexual orientations explored by your trans youth clients. Hopefully you will be excited to join them on their path of discovery and help them smooth out some of the bumps in the road.

Expect to feel inspired. My work with transgender youth and their families has been tremendously inspiring. I am moved to see these youth face what can at times seem like insurmountable challenges and dangers in order to be authentically themselves. I am touched by the parents who endeavor to open their minds about who their child is and face their fears for their child's safety and happiness.

For me, this work brings the same kind of excitement I experienced with my own coming out over 40 years ago. For some teens who are heading off to college and uneasy about leaving the safety of their home community and school, I have found it helpful to share a little about my own experiences. I try to communicate to them the excitement of pushing boundaries, being transgressive, demanding equal rights and celebrating difference. As I shift my work from clinical practice to training other clinicians and educators, I am happy to be part of a movement to make the world a safer and more welcoming place for all.

Expect to be challenged. You may find it difficult at first to see the person inside when their outward appearance and demeanor suggest a different gender then the one they disclose to you. It helps to use their affirmed name, along with pronouns and gendered language that they feel corresponds best to their gender. Each time you do so, you are reminding yourself of who they are, gradually overcoming the innate tendency to judge others' gender based on appearance. As you talk with them about their sexual and romantic attractions and behaviors you will learn about sexual orientations that may be new to you, such as asexual, biromantic, heteroflexible or pansexual. If you remain curious and open-minded, you are likely find the process personally expansive. As you accompany a number of transgender youth through various stages of transition, you will understand more deeply the dilemma they were in before transition. You will also see how joy and fulfillment can arise from pain and sadness, for youth and for their parents.

Examine any doubts you have about a youth's asserted gender identity. Pay attention to your doubts but don't let them overwhelm your ability to hear and trust what your client tells you. Let go of judgment about whether someone could pass easily as one gender or the other, and what it means if they do not care about passing. Separate your impressions of a young person's gender expression from your understanding of their gender. Transgender people, prior to asserting their gender, are socialized to act like typical boys or girls according to their assigned sex. For those whose authentic expression differs from these societal expectations, it can take a conscious effort to let go of learned behaviors and uncover the person inside. And do not expect a transgender person who is making a binary transition to dislike everything about their birth-assigned sex or the gendered parts of their physiology.

The intent of this book is to share essential information needed by experienced mental health clinicians who are expanding their practice to help transgender youth. But one book cannot provide you with everything you need to make this transition. I encourage you to look into the books, articles, blogs and videos listed at the end of each chapter, attend conferences, and seek out training offered by knowledgeable mental health clinicians.

I also encourage you to seek clinical supervision whenever you have a concern or a question about how to proceed. If you do not feel confident to make a medical referral decision and the youth is anxious for hormone treatment or surgery, seek consultation with a more experienced clinician. If you feel you may be moving ahead too quickly, or if your client has a complex mental health, substance abuse or family history, clinical supervision is warranted. If you are having difficulty maintaining a positive connection with a parent or advocating successfully at school, review the case with someone who has worked with numerous transgender teens or young adults and their parents or schools. Many clinicians seek guidance the first few times they work with transgender youth as their training did not include this subspecialty. If you are not aware of experienced clinicians in your area, the WPATH website's list of providers is a good place to start. You are not in this alone. This work is exciting and fulfilling. I hope you will find it as rewarding as I have.

APPENDICES

Glossary

Terminology used by and about transgender people is constantly invented and evolving. These definitions should be taken as my understanding of how these terms were most often used at the time this book was published.

Affirmed gender is the gender an individual declares themself* to be.

Someone who is **agender** considers themself* to be without gender.

An **asexual** person does not experience strong sexual attractions, but they may feel romantic attractions. For example, someone who considers themself* to be 'asexual, biromantic' feels romantically attracted to females and males but not sexually attracted to anyone.

Assigned sex, female or male, is determined at birth, based on the appearance of the baby's genitals.

Someone who is **bigender** considers themself* to be of two genders.

A **binder** is a garment used to flatten the chest. It helps the individual be less aware of their breasts and present with a more masculine body profile.

---

* 'Themself' is a variant of 'themselves' used by some individuals of non-binary gender identity.

A **biromantic** person is romantically attracted to females and males, but these feelings may not include sexual attraction.

Birth sex is the sex determined at birth based on the appearance of the baby's genitals.

A **bisexual** person is attracted to females and males.

Bottom surgeries include hysterectomy, orchiectomy and genital reconstruction surgeries.

Cisgender individuals are those whose assigned sex, gender identity and gender expression are either all male or all female. Can be shortened to **cis**.

Getting **clocked** is being perceived by others as transgender.

To be **closeted** is to keep one's LGBT identity secret.

To **come out** is to disclose one's LGBT identity to others.

Cross-sex hormones cause a male body to become more feminine or a female body to become more masculine.

Crossdressers wish to adopt the clothing and styles of grooming that is typical, in their culture, of the other sex.

Facial feminization is surgery to make a masculine face appear feminine.

A **female to male** (FTM) transgender person was assigned female at birth but feels male. He wants to be viewed by others as male.

A **gay** person is primarily or exclusively attracted to people of the same sex.

Gender affirmation surgeries include top surgery, breast augmentation, facial feminization surgery, trachea shave, hysterectomy, orchiectomy and genital reconstruction surgeries.

Gender dysphoria is a clinical term used to describe the unhappiness or distress caused by the conflict between gender identity and assigned sex or societal expectations for that sex.

Gender expression is a person's presentation of self to others as masculine, feminine, neither or both.

Gender identity is a person's inner sense of being female, male, neither or both.

Gender Identity Disorder is a mental health diagnosis that was previously used to describe transgender people. The category was changed to Gender Dysphoria in the most recent diagnostic manual.

Gender identity specialist is a mental health professional with expertise about gender identity and expression.

Gender nonconforming children are those whose desires, behaviors and manner do not conform to societal expectations for children of their assigned sex.

Genderfluid, **genderqueer** or **gender-neutral** people are those with a gender identity that is neither male nor female, or is a blend of male and female.

Genital reconstruction surgeries (GRS) are surgical procedures that alter a person's genitals to better fit their gender identity.

A **heteroflexible** person is a heterosexual who is open to sexual interactions with someone of the same sex.

A **heterosexual** person is attracted primarily or exclusively to people whose sex differs from theirs.

A **homosexual** person is attracted primarily or exclusively to people of the same sex.

Hysterectomy is surgical removal of the uterus.

An **intersex** person's physiology is not exclusively male or female.

A **lesbian** is a woman who is primarily or exclusively attracted to women.

LGBT is an abbreviation for lesbian, gay, bisexual and transgender. In **LGBTQ** the 'Q' stands for 'queer' or 'questioning.' **LGB** refers to lesbian, gay and bisexual.

A **male to female** (MTF) transgender person was assigned male at birth but feels female. She wants to be viewed by others as female.

Medical transition is the use of medical interventions, such as hormones or surgery, to alter a person's body to be more congruent with their gender identity.

Metoidioplasty is surgery to create a micro-penis by bringing the clitoris forward.

Microaggressions are casual instances of disrespect, insult or harassment, whether intentional or unintentional, toward members of a stigmatized group.

To **misgender** is to refer to someone by name, pronouns or gendered words (e.g., son, daughter) that do not fit with the individual's affirmed gender.

Natal sex is the sex determined at birth based on the appearance of the baby's genitals.

Nonaffirmation occurs when one's internal sense of gender identity is not affirmed by others.

Non-binary identities are those that fall outside binary sets of categories such as female/male, gay/straight and masculine/feminine. Some examples are: genderqueer, gender neutral, genderfluid, bisexual, pansexual, transmasculine and transfeminine.

Orchiectomy is surgical removal of the testicles.

Pangender and polygender people affirm a gender identity that encompasses more than female and male genders.

A **panromantic** person is romantically attracted to others without placing importance on the person's sex or gender. These feelings may not include sexual attraction.

Pansexual individuals feel sexual attraction toward others without placing importance on the partner's sex or gender.

Passing is the process of presenting oneself to be seen consistently as one's affirmed gender.

Phalloplasty is surgery to create a penis.

Puberty blockers are medical treatments that delay the onset of puberty or halt the progress of puberty.

Queer is a historically derogatory term that has been appropriated by the community for use in a prideful way. It is now an affirming umbrella term encompassing all with unconventional gender identity and/or sexuality.

Sex, female or male, is assigned at birth based on the appearance of the baby's genitals.

Sex reassignment surgery (SRS) is an older term for genital reconstruction surgery.

Sexuality refers to sexual feelings and behaviors.

Sexual orientation describes the relationship between a person's gender identity and the identities of those to whom that person is attracted. These include but are not limited to: gay, lesbian, bisexual, asexual, pansexual and heterosexual.

Social transition is when a transgender person begins presenting in public according to their gender identity rather than according to their assigned sex.

Stealth is living in one's affirmed gender without disclosing to others that one is trans.

Themself is the reflexive pronoun used by some non-binary individuals as part of the they/them/their pronoun set. Used to refer to one person, 'themself' fits better than 'themselves.'

Third-gender people affirm a gender identity other than female or male.

Top surgery is breast removal with male chest reconstruction.

Trachea shave is a surgical reduction in the Adam's apple.

Transfeminine individuals' gender identity and expression are in the female/feminine region of the spectrum but they do not necessarily identify as female.

Transgender, **trans**, or **trans*** people have a gender identity and/or gender expression that does not conform to their assigned sex. These are umbrella terms generally encompassing all who are not cisgender.

A **trans man** was assigned female at birth but feels male. He wants to be viewed by others as male.

Transmasculine individuals' gender identity and expression are in the male/masculine region of the spectrum but they do not necessarily identify as male.

Transphobia is fear of, or hostility toward, transgender people.

Transsexuals are people whose gender identity is in sharp contrast to their assigned sex. Many transgender individuals, especially teens and young adults, no longer use this term.

A **trans woman** was assigned male at birth but feels female. She wants to be viewed by others as female.

Vaginoplasty is surgery to create a vagina.

Organizations, Online Resources and Conferences

An updated list of resources and contact information for **Irwin Krieger** *can be found at* **www.CounselingTransgenderYouth.com**

SUPPORT GROUPS FOR YOUTH AND PARENTS

Gender Spectrum Lounge, online support groups: www.genderspectrum.org/lounge

Gendered Intelligence has support groups for youth in the United Kingdom: www.genderedintelligence.co.uk

Mermaids has support groups for parents in the United Kingdom: www.mermaidsuk.org.uk

PFLAG has meetings across the United States. To find a chapter near you: www.pflag.org/find-a-chapter

PFLAG Canada has chapters throughout Canada: www.pflagcanada.ca/pflag-chapters

Transcend Support lists support groups throughout Australia: www.transcendsupport.com.au

TransFamily (USA) hosts an email group for parents: www.transfamily.org/discussion.html

TransParent (USA) has chapters in a number of US locations: www.transparentusa.org

Trevor Space is a monitored peer networking site for LGBT youth ages 13–24: www.trevorspace.org

TRANSGENDER ADVOCACY

Asia-Pacific Transgender Network: www.weareaptn.org

Black Trans Advocacy (USA): www.blacktrans.org

CENESEX (Cuba): www.cenesex.org

FTM International: www.ftmi.org

Gender Centre, Inc. has a directory of resources in Australia: www.gendercentre.org.au

Gender Dynamix (South Africa): www.genderdynamix.org.za

Global Action for Trans* Equality: www.transactivists.org

Iranti-org (Africa): www.iranti-org.co.za

National Center for Transgender Equality (USA): www.transequality.org

OutRight Action International: www.outrightinternational.org

REDLACTRANS (Carribbean and Latin America): www.redlactrans.org.ar/site

Sahodari Foundation (India): www.sahodari.org

trans*formation (UK): www.transformationuk.com

Transgender Equality Network Ireland: www.teni.ie

Transgender Europe: tgeu.org

INTERSEX ADVOCACY

InterACT: www.interactadvocates.org

Organization Intersex International: www.oiiinternational.com

TRANSGENDER RESOURCES

FTM Information Resources: www.jotto.info/FTM/index.html

Hudson's FTM Resource Guide: www.ftmguide.org

Laura's Playground, with translation into many languages: www.lauras-playground.com

Transsexual and Transgender Road Map: www.tsroadmap.com

FAMILY AND SCHOOL ADVOCACY IN THE UNITED STATES

Campus Pride: www.campuspride.org

Gender Spectrum: www.genderspectrum.org

GLSEN: www.glsen.org

GSA Network: www.gsanetwork.org

transACTION – A Transgender Curriculum For Churches and Religious Institutions: www.welcomingresources.org/transgender.xml

TransKids Purple Rainbow Foundation: www.transkidspurplerainbow.org

Trans Youth Equality Foundation: www.transyouthequality.org

Trans Youth Family Allies: www.imatyfa.org

TransActive: www.transactiveonline.org

LEGAL ADVOCACY IN THE UNITED STATES

GLAD: www.glad.org

LLDEF: www.lambdalegal.org

National Center for Lesbian Rights:
www.nclrights.org/our-work/transgender-law

Sylvia Rivera Law Project: www.srlp.org

Transgender Law and Policy Institute:
www.transgenderlaw.org

Transgender Law Center: www.transgenderlawcenter.org

Transgender Legal Defense and Education Fund:
www.transgenderlegal.org

SUMMER CAMPS FOR TRANS YOUTH IN THE UNITED STATES

Camp Aranu'tiq (summer camp in New Hampshire and California): www.camparanutiq.org

Get Free (summer program for queer and trans youth of color in Oakland): www.bgdblog.org

Trans Youth Equality Foundation (summer and fall retreats in Maine): www.transyouthequality.org

ORGANIZATIONS COMBATING BULLYING AND STIGMA IN THE UNITED STATES

B Stigma Free: www.bstigmafree.org

Stop Bullying: www.stopbullying.gov

Tyler Clementi Foundation: www.tylerclementi.org

HEALTH INFORMATION

Australian and New Zealand Association for Transgender Health: www.anzpath.org

Center of Excellence for Transgender Health:
www.transhealth.ucsf.edu

European Professional Association for Transgender Health:
www.epath.eu

Fenway Center (list of transgender care providers in the USA):
www.transcaresite.org

Gender Identity Research and Education Society:
www.gires.org.uk

Transgender ASIA Research Centre: www.transgenderasia.org

Vancouver Coastal Health: www.transhealth.vch.ca

World Professional Association for Transgender Health:
www.wpath.org

PHONE AND ONLINE CRISIS SUPPORT FOR LGBT YOUTH

GLBT National Help Center (USA): glnh.org or 888-843-4564

Trans Lifeline: USA: (877) 565-8860 and Canada: (877) 330-6366.
www.translifeline.org

Trevor Project (USA): thetrevorproject.org (888-4-U-TREVOR)
is a confidential 24/7 crisis and suicide prevention helpline for
LGBT youth

Youthline (Canada): Open from 16:00–21:30 Sunday–Friday.
(Toronto time zone) Call: 800-268-9688. Text: 647-694-4275. TTY:
416-962-0777. Email: askus@youthline.ca. To chat, click the Chat
button at the top of this page: youthline.ca

CONFERENCES OUTSIDE THE UNITED STATES

**International Lesbian, Gay, Bisexual, Trans and Intersex
Association (ILGA)**: www.ilga.org

Sparkle: www.sparkle.org.uk

Trans*-Tagung Muenchen: www.transtagung-muenchen.com

Transguys.com keeps a comprehensive list of conferences in the United States and elsewhere

WPATH: See www.wpath.org for information on international and regional conferences

CONFERENCES IN THE UNITED STATES

Black Trans Advocacy, Dallas: www.blacktrans.org/conference/btac-welcome.html

First Event, Boston: www.firstevent.org

Gender Conference East: www.genderconferenceeast.org

Gender Infinity, Houston: www.genderinfinity.org

Gender Spectrum, California: www.genderspectrum.org

Gender Odyssey, Seattle: www.genderodyssey.org

Philadelphia Trans Health Conference: www.mazzonicenter.org/trans-health

Southern Comfort Conference: www.southerncomfortconference.org

Texas Transgender Nondiscrimination Summit: www.txtns.org

Transgender Lives, Connecticut: www.transadvocacy.org/transgender-lives-conference

Transgender Spectrum Conference, St. Louis: www.umsl.edu/~transgenderspectrum/

TransOhio Transgender and Ally Symposium: www.transohio.org

True Colors LGBT Youth Conference, Connecticut: www.ourtruecolors.org

Sample Letters

This appendix contains eight sample letters of referral for fictional clients of various ages and gender identities seeking hormone treatment or surgery. See my outline in the final section of Chapter 10 or 'Other outlines for writing referral letters' listed at the end of Chapter 10 for ideas. As you gain experience you will find your own way to structure a letter and decide what you feel is most important and appropriate to include. The letters in this section are as follows:

1. Referral for an initial assessment for future puberty blockers for a trans boy.
2. Referral for puberty blockers for a trans girl who is already in puberty.
3. Referral letters for a teen with non-binary gender identity:
   a. For cross-sex hormones.
   b. For top surgery the following year. *This sample letter includes a paragraph about non-binary identities that can be used if the insurance policy language implies that coverage is only for those undergoing binary gender transition.*
4. Referral letters for a trans male teen:
   a. For cross-sex hormones.
   b. For top surgery the following year.
5. Referral letters for a trans female young adult:
   a. For cross-sex hormones.
   b. For genital surgery two years later.

1. REFERRAL FOR AN INITIAL ASSESSMENT FOR FUTURE PUBERTY BLOCKERS FOR A TRANS BOY

March 30, 2016

RE: Monique 'Joshua' Wilson

DOB: 6/2/06

Dear Dr. Gordon,

I am referring Monique 'Joshua' Wilson to you for an initial consultation about future treatment with puberty blockers. Joshua is a 9-year-old trans boy in fourth grade. I am a clinical social worker in private practice with experience evaluating many transgender individuals regarding readiness for hormone treatment or surgery. Joshua and his family have met with me for assessment and psychotherapy since June 20, 2015.

Joshua told his parents in the summer of 2014 that he is a boy. He told me that he feels he has always been a boy. He never liked being called a girl or dressing as a girl.

Joshua made a social transition to male at school in January of 2015. His parents, his siblings and school staff have been fully supportive. His peers have been supportive with the exception of a few who are unkind to others as well. He was bullied by some boys in his class and felt depressed with occasional suicide thoughts but no urge or intent to harm himself. When his parents alerted his teacher about the harassment, the school intervened, with partial success, in the latter half of third grade. This year, Joshua is not being harassed and as a result he is not stressed at school. He uses the boys' bathroom without incident.

Joshua is anxious by nature, but not to a degree that interferes with his functioning. He comes across as an exuberant and charming youngster. Since making his transition, Joshua likes being transgender and likes being treated as a boy.

Joshua understands the purpose of puberty blockers, as well as the need to wait for the onset of puberty to be treated with blockers. His pediatrician has explained to him what the early signs of puberty are. He is interested in receiving treatment to block puberty when it is appropriate. Based on his history so far, if he expresses discomfort at the onset of puberty about the initial and anticipated changes of puberty, I recommend puberty blocking treatment at that time. At that point he would meet the criteria for puberty suppressing hormones in the WPATH *Standards of Care*. His *DSM-5* diagnosis is Childhood Gender Dysphoria (F64.2).

I am referring Joshua to you now so you can meet him and his parents, coordinate with his pediatrician to monitor changes, and intervene when appropriate. Joshua's parents are in agreement with this plan. He will continue in psychotherapy with me.

Please call me if you need any additional information or if you would like to discuss Monique 'Joshua' Wilson's treatment with me.

Sincerely,

2. REFERRAL FOR PUBERTY BLOCKERS FOR A TRANS GIRL WHO IS ALREADY IN PUBERTY

March 4, 2015

RE: Ethan Foster

DOB: 2/15/02

Dear Dr. Diaz,

I am writing to recommend that you evaluate Ethan Foster for endocrine treatment to postpone puberty. I am a clinical social worker in private practice with experience evaluating many transgender teens and adults regarding readiness for hormone treatment or surgery. Ethan and her parents have an appointment to see you on March 18. Her *DSM-5* diagnosis is Adolescent Gender Dysphoria (F64.1).

Ethan is a 13-year-old seventh grader who was assigned male at birth. She has always engaged in gender atypical play and affiliated with girls. For the past eight months she has been thinking about gender intently. She watches videos of young adults transitioning and identifies with the feelings they express. Sometimes she imagines herself as a teenage girl and feels frustrated about living as a boy. She disclosed her female gender identity to her parents during her December school vacation. She was surprised and pleased with their open-minded response.

After an initial meeting with Ethan's parents on January 7, 2015, I have met with Ethan, alone and with her parents on five occasions. Mr. and Mrs. Foster have gathered information online and in discussion with me. They are in full support of Ethan starting on puberty blockers now as she is well into her puberty.

Ethan is comfortable keeping her male name and pronouns for now, although she prefers that we refer to her with female pronouns in the privacy of family sessions. She is slowly trying out female presentation at home. Her siblings are aware and supportive.

Ethan and her parents understand the purpose of this treatment is to block further puberty and possibly transition to female later on. I have discussed fertility consequences and the option of sperm banking with Ethan and her parents.

Having met with Ethan and her parents for a total of six sessions over the past two months, I see her as a transgender teen appropriately seeking treatment to block puberty, with full parental support. She meets the WPATH *Standards of Care* for puberty blocking treatment, which is necessary for her well-being. She and her parents intend for her to continue in therapy with me for support through this process. I am writing to recommend that you help Ethan Foster and her parents with their request for an evaluation for puberty blocking treatment. I have discussed this treatment plan with Ethan's pediatrician.

Please call me if you need any additional information or if you would like to discuss Ethan's treatment with me.

Sincerely,

3A. REFERRAL FOR CROSS-SEX HORMONES FOR A TEEN WITH NON-BINARY GENDER IDENTITY

September 22, 2014

RE: Emma 'Kayden' Lewis

DOB: 7/14/97

Dear Dr. Diaz,

I have referred Emma 'Kayden' Lewis to you for evaluation for hormone treatment. Kayden has been seeing me for assessment and psychotherapy since October 7, 2013. I am a clinical social worker in private practice with experience evaluating many transgender teens and adults regarding readiness for hormone treatment or surgery. Kayden is a 17-year-old with a non-binary gender identity. Kayden prefers they/them/their pronouns. Their diagnosis is Adolescent Gender Dysphoria (*DSM-5* Diagnosis: F64.1). Kayden was assigned female at birth. Since puberty, Kayden has been uncomfortable with others perceiving them as female. For the past 18 months Kayden has identified as gender neutral, disclosing to their parents and their former therapist about a year ago.

Over the past few years Kayden has experienced intermittent depression and persistent social anxiety, leading to a referral two years ago to Maureen Nesbit, LCSW [Licensed Clinical Social Worker] for psychotherapy. Therapy has been somewhat helpful while various trials of antidepressant medication did not alleviate depression or anxiety. Kayden has felt more confident and has had less social anxiety since making a social transition at school in January. Kayden has consistently reminded others to use their affirmed name and 'they' pronouns. Kayden's parents have remarked to me that Kayden seems much happier and interacts more with peers and adults since then.

Kayden has been using a binder to present a more gender-neutral (i.e., not female) profile. They are especially uncomfortable when they see themself in the mirror and conclude that others will see them as female. Kayden has also expressed an interest in having a deeper voice as they believe it would be more comfortable to be mistaken as male than as female. Kayden realizes it is highly unlikely that others will spontaneously view them as gender neutral outside of specific gender-identity-aware contexts. Kayden is interested in cross-gender hormone treatment for the purpose of lowering their voice. We discussed that this could be done on a 3–6-month basis and reassessed, as changes other than voice tend to be minimal during the early period of testosterone treatment. The vocal changes would be gradual, could be interrupted but not reversed, and decisions about further masculinization could be made on the basis of Kayden's responses to these early changes. I believe this approach fits with Kayden's current needs and gender identity. Given Kayden's distress about being viewed by others as female, and their persistent expression of non-binary gender identity and discomfort with a female-sounding voice, it is my opinion that this request meets the WPATH *Standards of Care*, which recommend individually determined decisions, especially for adolescents.

Kayden has met with me for 19 sessions to date. Six of these sessions included one or both parents. I met with the parents alone for one session. I have spoken with Maureen Nesbit and Kayden's pediatrician about the referral for hormones. I see Kayden as a mentally stable individual appropriately seeking treatment with male hormones for increased concordance between their physiology and their non-binary gender identity. They are able to give informed consent for this treatment. Kayden's parents are in accord with this plan. Kayden meets the *Standards of Care* for cross-gender hormone treatment, which is necessary for their well-being. They intend to continue in psychotherapy with me for support through this process. I am writing to recommend that you help Emma 'Kayden' Lewis with their request for an evaluation for hormone treatment.

Please call me if you need any additional information or if you would like to discuss Kayden's treatment with me.

Sincerely,

3B. REFERRAL FOR TOP SURGERY THE FOLLOWING YEAR FOR THE SAME YOUTH WITH NON-BINARY GENDER IDENTITY

This sample letter includes a paragraph about non-binary identities that can be used if the insurance policy language implies that coverage is only for those undergoing binary gender transition.

July 19, 2015

RE: Kayden Lewis

DOB: 7/14/97

Dear Dr. Morgan,

I am writing to support Kayden Lewis's request for breast removal and male chest reconstruction for the purpose of gender transition. I have been seeing Kayden for assessment and psychotherapy since October 7, 2013. I am a clinical social worker in private practice with experience evaluating many transgender teens and adults regarding readiness for hormone treatment or surgery. Kayden is an 18-year-old with a non-binary gender identity. Kayden prefers they/them/their pronouns. Their diagnosis is Gender Dysphoria (*DSM-5* Diagnosis: F64.1).

Kayden was assigned female at birth. Since puberty, Kayden has been uncomfortable with others perceiving them as female. For over two years, Kayden has identified as gender neutral. The wording of the criteria listed in the *DSM-5* diagnosis of Gender Dysphoria clearly indicates that non-binary gender identities are included. Similarly, the section on surgery in the WPATH *Standards of Care* contains language inclusive of non-binary identities: 'While many transsexual, transgender, and gender-nonconforming individuals find comfort with their gender identity, role and expression without surgery, for many others surgery is essential and medically necessary to alleviate their gender dysphoria.'

Over the past few years, Kayden has experienced intermittent depression and persistent social anxiety, leading to a referral for psychotherapy with Maureen Nesbit, LCSW. Therapy was somewhat helpful, while various trials of antidepressant medication did not alleviate depression or anxiety. Kayden felt more confident and had less social anxiety after making a social transition at school in January of 2014. Kayden's parents have both remarked to me that Kayden seems much happier and interacts more with peers and adults since then.

Kayden has been using a binder to present a more gender-neutral (i.e., not female) profile. They are especially uncomfortable when they see themself in the mirror and conclude that others will see them as female. Kayden also expressed an interest in having a deeper voice as they believed they would be more comfortable if mistaken as male than as female. In September of 2014, I referred Kayden to Dr. Diaz for cross-gender hormone treatment. We discussed that this could be done on a 3–6-month basis and reassessed, as changes other than voice tend to be minimal during the early period of testosterone treatment. Kayden met with Dr. Diaz and started testosterone injections in October. As Kayden expected, they are relieved to have a lower voice from hormone treatment. In addition, Kayden is pleased with the additional masculinization from testosterone and wants to continue hormone treatment. Kayden's parents note that Kayden is more confident and outgoing since their voice has deepened. As a result the parents felt fully confident of Kayden's gender-neutral identity and supported a legal name change to 'Kayden' a few months ago.

Kayden is mentally stable, and has given a great deal of thought to making this transition, with a consistent intention to have their breasts removed. They have the mental capacity to make a fully informed decision regarding surgery. Based on Kayden's progress with social transition and hormone treatment, Kayden's parents are fully in support of top surgery at this time. Kayden will be attending college in the fall so they are hoping the surgery can be scheduled at the start of winter break. I am writing to recommend that Kayden

Lewis is fully prepared for top surgery. They have fulfilled the WPATH *Standards of Care* for gender transition surgery. This surgery is necessary for their well-being at this time.

Please contact me if you have any questions about my evaluation of Kayden not answered in this letter.

Sincerely,

4A. REFERRAL FOR CROSS-SEX HORMONES
FOR A TRANS MALE TEEN

June 2, 2013

RE: Owen Parker

DOB: 3/19/98

Dear Dr. Harris,

I am referring Owen Parker to you for evaluation for hormone treatment. Owen has been seeing me for assessment since March 4, 2013. He is a 15-year-old FTM ninth-grade student. His *DSM-5* diagnosis is Adolescent Gender Dysphoria (F64.1). I am a clinical social worker in private practice with experience evaluating many transgender teens and adults regarding readiness for hormone treatment or surgery.

Owen was assigned female at birth. He has always been a tomboy and didn't fit in with girls. He came out as lesbian in sixth grade, but then realized that he did not want to label himself by gender or sexual orientation. He cut his hair short and dressed androgynously. Hearing his female name and pronouns made him uncomfortable. His parents could see he was becoming more isolated from peers and less motivated for school. They took him to see a therapist, Regina Quinley PhD, who was known to be LGBT-friendly. Owen was able to gain more clarity about his identity as he talked at length with her, but his depression did not improve. Dr. Quinley referred him to Eugene Campbell, APRN [Advanced Practice Registered Nurse], who prescribed antidepressant medication for Owen, which helped improve mood somewhat.

In the spring of 2012, Owen came out to his friends as transgender. A few months later he came out to his parents and started wearing a binder. His parents agreed to his request for a legal name change. He made a full social transition last summer. His grades have improved this year and his parents find him to be a more authentic, happy and interactive teenager. Owen has told his parents and Dr. Quinley that he would like to begin treatment with testosterone. Dr. Quinley, while confident of Owen's affirmed male identity, recommended he meet with me for evaluation as she has not previously referred anyone for hormone treatment.

Owen has met with me for six sessions to date. The first and last session included his parents. The parents also met with me once without Owen. I have spoken with Dr. Quinley as well as with Eugene Campbell, who continues to prescribe [name of medication] for Owen.

I see Owen as a mentally stable transgender adolescent appropriately seeking treatment with male hormones for gender transition. He is able to give informed consent for this treatment. He meets the WPATH *Standards of Care* for cross-sex hormone treatment, which is necessary for his well-being. He intends to continue in psychotherapy with Dr. Quinley for support through this process. He and his parents will consult with me as needed. Owen's parents are in support of this treatment plan.

I am writing to recommend that you help Owen Parker with his request for an evaluation for hormone treatment. Owen and his parents are interested in any information you can provide about egg harvesting as they are aware that hormone treatment may lead to infertility.

Please call me if you need any additional information or if you would like to discuss Owen's treatment with me.

Sincerely,

4B. REFERRAL FOR TOP SURGERY FOR THE SAME TEEN, THE FOLLOWING YEAR

April 9, 2014

RE: Owen Parker

DOB: 3/19/98

Dear Dr. Morgan,

I am writing to support Owen Parker's request for breast removal and male chest reconstruction for the purpose of gender transition. Owen initially met with me for six sessions, including two with his parents, beginning March 4, 2013. He is a 16-year-old FTM tenth-grade student. His *DSM-5* diagnosis is Adolescent Gender Dysphoria (F64.1). Owen was assigned female at birth. He has always been a tomboy and didn't fit in with girls. He came out as lesbian in sixth grade, but then realized that he did not want to label himself by gender or sexual orientation. He cut his hair short and dressed androgynously. Hearing his female name and pronouns made him uncomfortable. His parents could see he was becoming more isolated from peers and less motivated for school. They took him to see a therapist, Regina Quinley PhD, who was known to be LGBT-friendly. Owen was able to gain more clarity about his identity as he talked at length with her. She also referred him to Eugene Campbell, APRN, who prescribed antidepressant medication, which has been helpful with mood.

In 2012, Owen came out to his friends and his parents. He made a social transition and started wearing a binder. His parents agreed to his request for a legal name change. Owen told his parents and Dr. Quinley that he would like to begin treatment with testosterone. Dr. Quinley recommended he meet with me for evaluation as she has not previously referred anyone for hormone treatment. I referred Owen to Dr. Harris (endocrinologist) in June of 2013 for cross-sex hormone treatment.

Owen has been taking male hormones since July of 2013, prescribed by Dr. Harris. He is more comfortable having a deeper voice. He is pleased that he is generally seen by others as male. Eugene Campbell has reduced his dose of [name of medication] to X mg per day. His mood has remained stable. Owen is seeking top surgery to feel more confident and congruent in his male presentation. He is looking forward to being free of a binder, especially in the summer heat. His parents are in support of top surgery as a next step. Owen has continued meeting with Dr. Quinley since starting testosterone and in addition met with me every 6–8 weeks regarding his progress with gender transition. Dr. Quinley and Owen's parents support the referral for top surgery.

Owen has met with me for 12 sessions to date. Three sessions included his parents and there was one additional session for the parents only. Owen is mentally healthy and stable, and has given a great deal of thought to making this transition, with a consistent intention to have his breasts removed. He has the mental capacity to make a fully informed decision regarding surgery. I am writing to recommend that Owen Parker is fully prepared for top surgery. He has fulfilled the WPATH *Standards of Care* for gender affirmation surgery. This surgery is necessary for his well-being.

Sincerely,

5A. REFERRAL FOR CROSS-SEX HORMONE TREATMENT FOR A TRANS FEMALE YOUNG ADULT

April 9, 2012

RE: Carlos Martinez

DOB: 2/17/93

Dear Dr. Harris,

I am referring Carlos Martinez to you for evaluation for hormone treatment. Carlos has been seeing me for assessment and psychotherapy since June 4, 2011. I am a clinical social worker in private practice with experience evaluating many transgender teens and adults regarding readiness for hormone treatment or surgery. Carlos is a 19-year-old transgender woman. Her *DSM-5* diagnosis is Gender Dysphoria (F64.1). She has not yet chosen a female name.

Carlos was assigned male at birth. She does not recall thinking about gender as a child. For the past few years, she has been researching transgender identities online. Carlos first disclosed her transgender identity to a friend two years ago. She is currently living with her parents and working in a supermarket.

When she first met with me, Carlos described herself as female with some traditionally masculine interests, such as carpentry. She has felt awkward trying out a fully female presentation, as she is very tall. Over the months we have been meeting she has gradually adopted a more androgynous presentation. On a number of occasions she has gone out with friends presenting fully as female. This has confirmed her sense of being female. She recently started laser treatment for facial hair removal.

Carlos has disclosed her female gender identity to her parents, her brother and her friends. All but her father have responded supportively. Father has met with me twice. He continues to disapprove, mostly on religious grounds, but accepts that Carlos has taken some time in therapy to understand herself fully and is choosing now to begin medical transition.

Carlos has met with me for 21 sessions to date. I see her as a mentally stable transgender woman appropriately seeking treatment with female hormones for gender transition. She is able to give informed consent for this treatment. She intends to continue in psychotherapy with me for support through this process. I am writing to recommend that you help Carlos Martinez with her request for an evaluation for hormone treatment. She meets the WPATH *Standards of Care* for hormone treatment, which is necessary for her well-being at this time.

Carlos smokes cigarettes. She is aware of the risks of smoking while taking estrogen. I have urged her to reduce and then stop smoking, but she has been inconsistent about this so far.

Please call me if you need any additional information or if you would like to discuss Carlos's treatment with me.

Sincerely,

5B: REFERRAL FOR GENITAL SURGERY FOR THE SAME YOUNG ADULT, TWO YEARS LATER

May 17, 2014

RE: Alicia Martinez

DOB: 2/17/93

Dear Dr. Walker,

I am writing to support Alicia Martinez's request for Genital Reconstruction Surgery (GRS) with you. I have been seeing Alicia since June 4, 2011 for evaluation and psychotherapy. Alicia is a 21-year-old transgender woman. Her *DSM-5* diagnosis is Gender Dysphoria (F64.1). I am a clinical social worker in private practice with experience evaluating many transgender teens and adults regarding readiness for hormone treatment or surgery.

Alicia was assigned male at birth. She does not recall thinking about gender as a child. As a teen, she learned about transgender identities online. Alicia first disclosed her transgender identity to a friend in 2010. When she first met with me, Alicia felt awkward trying out a fully female presentation, as she is very tall. She gradually adopted a more androgynous presentation and on a number of occasions she went out with friends presenting fully as female. This confirmed her sense of being female. While Alicia's mother, brother and friends were supportive when she disclosed her female identity, her father continues to disapprove, mostly on religious grounds.

In April of 2012 I referred Alicia to Dr. Harris for cross-sex hormone treatment. After six months of hormone treatment Alicia felt comfortable making a full social transition. Alicia used to smoke cigarettes. She was able to stop smoking after a few failed attempts. She legally changed her name to Alicia. Alicia works at a supermarket. While she was worried about how her co-workers would respond to her transition, store management was supportive and her co-workers were respectful. Alicia has long been interested in carpentry. She recently started working part-time for a friend of her father who owns a construction business. Her father's views toward her gender transition have softened as he sees his friend accept Alicia as a woman.

Alicia has met with me steadily since 2011, most recently on a monthly basis. I see her as a mentally stable transgender woman appropriately seeking GRS, which is necessary for her well-being. She is seeking genital surgery to feel more fully congruent and for possible future sexual intimacy. She is able to give informed consent for this surgery. She intends to continue in psychotherapy with me for support through this process. I am writing to recommend that you help Alicia with her request for GRS. She meets the WPATH *Standards of Care* for GRS.

Please call me if you need any additional information or if you would like to discuss Alicia's treatment with me.

Sincerely,

References

ABC News *20/20* documentary (2012) 'Boys Will Be Girls.' New York, NY: ABC TV. Accessed on 3/1/17 at www.youtube.com/watch?v=u-DjtvAPOhE.

Abeni, C. (2015) 'San Diego mourns fourth trans teen lost to suicide this year.' *The Advocate*, online edition, October 7, 2015. Accessed on 3/1/17 at www.advocate. com/transgender/2015/10/07/san-diego-mourns-fourth-trans-teen-lost-suicide-year.

American Psychiatric Association (2000) *Diagnostic and Statistical Manual of Mental Disorders* (4th edn). Washington, DC: American Psychiatric Association Publishing.

American Psychiatric Association (2013) *Diagnostic and Statistical Manual of Mental Disorders* (5th edn). Washington, DC: American Psychiatric Association Publishing.

Andrews, A. with Lyon, J. (2014) *Some Assembly Required: The Not-So-Secret Life of a Transgender Teen*. New York, NY: Simon and Schuster.

Attwood, T. (2015) *The Complete Guide to Asperger's Syndrome* (revised edn). Philadelphia, PA: Jessica Kingsley Publishers.

Australian Government (2013) *Guidelines on the Recognition of Sex and Gender*. Canberra: Australian Government. Accessed on 3/1/17 at www.ag.gov.au/Publications/Documents/Australian GovernmentGuidelinesontheRecognitionofSexandGender/ AustralianGovernmentGuidelinesontheRecognitionofSexandGender.PDF.

Baker, J. (2015) 'The son who wasn't.' *Psychology Today 48*, 5, 44–46.

Beam, C. (2007) *Transparent: Love, Family and Living the T with Transgender Teenagers*. New York, NY: Harcourt, Inc.

Beemyn. G. and Rankin, S. (2011) *The Lives of Transgender People*. New York, NY: Columbia University Press.

Bieber, I., Dain, H.J., Dince, P.R., Drellich, M.G. *et al.* (1962) *Homosexuality: A Psychoanalytic Study of Male Homosexuals*. New York, NY: Basic Books.

Brill, S. and Pepper, R. (2008) *The Transgender Child: A Handbook for Families and Professionals*. San Francisco, CA: Cleis Press.

Butler, J. (2006) 'Undiagnosing Gender.' In P. Currah, R.M. Juang and S.P. Minter (eds) *Transgender Rights*. Minneapolis, MN: University of Minneapolis Press.

Canadian Pediatric Endocrine Group. (March, 2012) 'Pubertal blockade safe for pediatric patients with gender identity disorder.' *EndocrineToday*, online edition. Accessed on 3/1/17 at www.healio.com/endocrinology/pediatric-endocrinology/news/print/endocrine-today/%7B69c4c36a-37c3-4053-a856-22a27f8df62c%7D/pubertal-blockade-safe-for-pediatric-patients-with-gender-identity-disorder.

Carastathis, A. (2014) 'The concept of intersectionality in feminist theory.' *Philosophy Compass 9*, 5, 304–314.

Carmel, T., Hopwood, R. and dickey, l.m. (2014) 'Mental Health Concerns.' In L. Erickson-Schroth (ed.) *Trans Bodies, Trans Selves*. New York, NY: Oxford University Press.

Chen, D., Hidalgo, M., Leibowitz, S., Leininger, J. *et al.* (2016) 'Multidisciplinary care for gender-diverse youth: A narrative review and unique model of gender-affirming care.' *Transgender Health 1*, 1, 117–123.

Chyten-Brennan, J. (2014) 'Surgical Transition.' In L. Erickson-Schroth (ed.) *Trans Bodies, Trans Selves*. New York, NY: Oxford University Press.

Cochran, B.N., Peavy, K.M. and Robohm, J.S. (2007) 'Do specialized services exist for LGBT individuals seeking treatment for substance misuse? A study of available treatment programs.' *Substance Use and Misuse 42*, 1, 161–176.

Cohen-Kettenis, P.T. and Pfäffln, F. (2003) *Transgenderism and Intersexuality in Childhood and Adolescence: Making Choices*. Thousand Oaks, CA: Sage Publications.

Cohen-Kettenis, P.T., Schagen, S.E.E., Steensma, T.D., de Vries, A.L.C. and Delemarre-van de Waal, H.A. (2011) 'Puberty suppression in a gender-dysphoric adolescent: A 22-year follow-up.' *Archives of Sexual Behavior 40*, 4, 843–847.

Coleman, E., Bockting, W., Botzer, M., Cohen-Kettenis, P. *et al.* (2011) 'Standards of care for the health of transsexual, transgender, and gender-nonconforming people, version 7.' *International Journal of Transgenderism 13*, 4, 165–232.

Conron, K.J., Scott, G., Stowell, G.S. and Landers, S.J. (2012) 'Transgender health in Massachusetts: Results from a household probability sample of adults.' *American Journal of Public Health 102*, 1, 118–122.

Cotten, T.T. (ed.) (2012) *Hung Jury: Testimonies of Genital Surgery by Transsexual Men*. Oakland, CA: Transgress Press.

Crawford, N. (2003) 'Understanding children's atypical gender behavior: A model support group helps parents learn to accept and affirm their gender-variant children.' *Monitor on Psychology 34*, 8, 40–42.

Curtis R., Martin, J., Wylie, K., Reed, T. and Reed, B. (2015) *A Guide to Lower Surgery for Those Assigned Female, Identifying as Men, Trans Masculine, Non-Binary or Non-Gender*. Ashtead, Surrey, England: The Gender Identity Research and Education Society.

Dahl, M., Feldman, J., Goldberg, J.M. and Jaberi, A. (2006) 'Physical aspects of transgender endocrine therapy.' *International Journal of Transgenderism 9*, 3/4, 111–134.

Davies, S. and Goldberg, J.M. (2006) 'Clinical aspects of transgender speech feminization and masculinization.' *International Journal of Transgenderism 9*, 3/4, 167–196.

Davies, S., Papp, V.G. and Antoni, C. (2015) 'Voice and communication change for gender nonconforming individuals: Giving voice to the person inside.' *International Journal of Transgenderism 16*, 3, 117–159.

Davis, S.A. and Meier, S.C. (2013) 'Effects of testosterone treatment and chest reconstruction surgery on mental health and sexuality in female-to-male transgender people.' *International Journal of Sexual Health 26*, 2, 133–128.

D'Emilio, J. (1992) 'Foreword.' In K. Jay and A. Young (eds) *Out of the Closets: Voices of Gay Liberation* (20th anniversary edn). New York, NY: New York University Press.

Deutsch, M. (2013) 'Use of the informed consent model in the provision of cross-sex hormone therapy: A survey of the practices of selected clinics.' *International Journal of Transgenderism 13*, 3, 140–146.

Deutsch, M. (2014) 'Medical Transition.' In L. Erickson-Schroth (ed.) *Trans Bodies, Trans Selves*. New York, NY: Oxford University Press.

Deutsch, M. (2016) *Overview of Feminizing Hormone Therapy*. San Francisco, CA: Center of Excellence for Transgender Health, University of California. Accessed on 3/1/17 at http://transhealth.ucsf.edu/tcoe?page=guidelines-feminizing-therapy.

de Vries, A.L.C., Cohen-Kettenis P.T. and Delemarre-van de Waal, H. (2006) 'Clinical management of gender dysphoria in adolescents.' *International Journal of Transgenderism 9*, 3/4, 83–94.

de Vries, A.L.C., McGuire, J.K., Steensma, T.D., Wagenaar, E.C.F., Doreleijers, T.A.H. and Cohen-Kettenis, P.T. (2014) 'Young adult psychological outcome after puberty suppression and gender reassignment.' *Pediatrics 134*, 4, 696–704.

de Vries, A.L.C., Noens, I.L.J., Cohen-Kettenis, P.T., van Berckelaer-Onnes, I.A. and Doreleijers, T.A. (2010) 'Autism spectrum disorders in gender dysphoric children and adolescents.' *Journal of Autism and Developmental Disorders 40*, 930–936.

Diamond, M. (2006) 'Biased-interaction theory of psychosexual development: "How does one know if one is male or female?"' *Sex Roles 55*, 9/10, 589–600.

Diamond, M. and Beh, H. (2008) 'Changes in the management of children with intersex conditions.' *Nature Clinical Practice, Endocrinology and Metabolism 4*, 1, 4–5.

Dodge, A., Burke, B.Z. and Oransky, M. (2016) 'Addressing Suicidality in Gender Expansive Youth.' Presentation at Gender East Conference, Newark, NJ, November 11, 2016.

Drescher, J. and Pula, J. (2014) 'Ethical issues raised by the treatment of gender-variant prepubescent children.' *LGBT Bioethics: Visibility, Disparities, and Dialogue (special report), Hastings Center Report 44*, 5, S17–S22.

Ehrensaft, D. (2011) *Gender Born, Gender Made: Raising Healthy Gender-Nonconforming Children*. New York, NY: The Experiment.

Ehrensaft, D. (2012) 'From gender identity disorder to gender identity creativity: True gender self child therapy.' *Journal of Homosexuality 59*, 3, 337–356.

Ehrensaft, D. (2016) *The Gender Creative Child: Pathways for Nurturing and Supporting Children Who Live Outside of Gender Boxes*. New York, NY: The Experiment.

Epps, G. (2016) 'North Carolina's Bathroom Bill is a constitutional monstrosity.' *The Atlantic*, online, May 10, 2016. Accessed 3/1/17 at www.theatlantic.com/politics/archive/2016/05/hb2-is-a-constitutional-monstrosity/482106.

Erickson-Schroth, L. (2013) 'Update on the biology of transgender identity.' *Journal of Gay and Lesbian Mental Health 17*, 2, 150–174.

Erikson, E. (1968) *Identity, Youth and Crisis*. New York, NY: W.W. Norton.

Ettner, R. (1996) *Confessions of a Gender Defender: A Psychologist's Reflections on Life among the Transgendered*. Chicago, IL: Chicago Spectrum Press.

Fausto-Sterling, A. (2000) *Sexing the Body: Gender Politics and the Construction of Sexuality*. New York, NY: Basic Books.

Finken, L. (2009) '"What should I do?" How consultants impact adolescents' risky decisions.' *The Prevention Researcher 16*, 2, 12–16.

GIRES (2016) *Lower Surgery for Those Assigned Male, Who Identify as Trans Women, Trans Feminine, Non-Binary or Non-Gender*. Ashtead, Surrey, England: The Gender Identity Research and Education Society.

GLSEN (2016) *The 2015 National School Climate Survey: Executive Summary*. Accessed on 3/23/17 at www.glsen.org/article/2015-national-school-climate-survey.

Gómez-Gil, E., Zubiaurre-Elorza, L., Esteva, I., Guillamon, A. *et al.* (2012) 'Hormone-treated transsexuals report less social distress, anxiety and depression.' *Psychoneuroendocrinology 37*, 5, 662–70.

Gray, S.A.O., Carter, A.S. and Levitt, H. (2012) 'A critical review of assumptions about gender variant children in psychological research.' *Journal of Gay and Lesbian Mental Health 16*, 1, 4–30.

Green, J. (2004) *Becoming a Visible Man*. Nashville, TN: Vanderbilt University Press.

Griffin, P. (2015) *Developing Policies for Transgender Students on High School Teams*. Indianapolis, IN: National Federation of State High School Associations. Accessed on 3/1/17 at www.nfhs.org/articles/developing-policies-for-transgender-students-on-high-school-teams.

Grossman, A.H. and D'Augelli, R.D. (2006) 'Transgender youth: Invisible and vulnerable.' *Journal of Homosexuality 51*, 1, 111–128.

Hastings, J. (2016) *Approach to Genderqueer, Gender Non-Conforming, and Gender Nonbinary People*. San Francisco, CA: Center of Excellence for Transgender Health, University of California. Accessed on 3/1/17 at http://transhealth.ucsf.edu/trans?page=guidelines-gender-nonconforming.

Hembree, W.C., Cohen-Kettenis, P., Delemarre-van de Waal, H.A., Gooren, L.J. *et al.* (2009) 'Endocrine treatment of transsexual persons: An Endocrine Society clinical practice guideline.' *Journal of Clinical Endocrinology and Metabolism 94*, 9, 3132–3154.

Hendricks, M.L. and Testa, R.J. (2012) 'A conceptual framework for clinical work with transgender and gender nonconforming clients: An adaptation of the Minority Stress Model.' *Professional Psychology: Research and Practice 43*, 5, 460–467.

Hidalgo, M., Ehrensaft, D., Tishelman, A.C., Clark, L.F. *et al.* (2013) 'The gender affirmative model: What we know and what we aim to learn.' *Human Development 56*, 5, 285–290.

Hill, K.R. with Schrag, A. (2014) *Rethinking Normal: A Memoir in Transition*. New York, NY: Simon and Schuster.

Hill-Meyer, T. and Scarborough, D. (2014) 'Sexuality.' In L. Erickson-Schroth (ed.) *Trans Bodies, Trans Selves*. New York, NY: Oxford University Press.

Holman, C.W. and Goldberg, J. M. (2006) 'Ethical, legal, and psychosocial issues in care of transgender adolescents.' *International Journal of Transgenderism 9*, 3/4, 95–110.

Horn, S.S. and Romeo, K.E. (2010) 'Peer contexts for lesbian, gay, bisexual and transgender students: Reducing stigma, prejudice, and discrimination.' *The Prevention Researcher 17*, 4, 7–10.

Hoshiai, M., Matsumoto, Y., Sato, T., Ohnishi, M. *et al.* (2010) 'Psychiatric comorbidity among patients with gender identity disorder.' *Psychiatry and Clinical Neurosciences 64*, 5, 514–519.

Jacobs, L.A., Rachlin, K., Erickson-Schroth, L. and Janssen, A. (2014) 'Gender dysphoria and co-occurring autism spectrum disorders: Review, case examples, and treatment considerations.' *LGBT Health 1*, 4, 277–282.

Janssen, A., Huang, H. and Duncan, C. (2016) 'Gender variance among youth with autism spectrum disorders: A retrospective chart review.' *Transgender Health 1*, 1, 63–68.

Jay, K. and Young, A. (eds) (1992) *Out of the Closets: Voices of Gay Liberation* (20th anniversary edn). New York, NY: New York University Press.

Jennings, J. (2016) *Being Jazz: My Life as a (Transgender) Teen*. New York, NY: Crown Books for Young Readers.

Kailey, M. (2005) *Just Add Hormones: An Insider's Guide to the Transsexual Experience*. Boston, MA: Beacon Press.

Keo-Meier, C. and Hicks, L. (2014) 'Youth.' In L. Erickson-Schroth (ed.) *Trans Bodies, Trans Selves*. New York, NY: Oxford University Press.

King, R.S., Brown, G.R. and McCrea, C.R. (2011) 'Voice parameters that result in identification or misidentification of biological gender in male-to-female transgender veterans.' *International Journal of Transgenderism 13*, 3, 117–130.

Krieger, I. (2011) *Helping Your Transgender Teen: A Guide for Parents*. New Haven, CT: Genderwise Press.

Krieger, N. (2011) *Nina Here nor There: My Journey beyond Gender*. Boston, MA: Beacon Press.

Kuklin, S. (2014) *Beyond Magenta: Transgender Teens Speak Out*. Somerville, MA: Candlewick Press.

Kuvalanka, K.A., Weiner, J. L. and Mahan, D. (2014) 'Child, family and community transformations: Findings from interviews with mothers of transgender girls.' *Journal of GLBT Family Studies 10*, 4, 354–379.

Lev, A.I. (2004) *Transgender Emergence: Therapeutic Guidelines for Working with Gender-Variant People and Their Families*. New York, NY: Haworth Clinical Practice Press.

Malpas, J. (2011) 'Between pink and blue: A multi-dimensional family approach to gender nonconforming children and their families.' *Family Process 50*, 4, 453–470.

May, T., Pang, K. and Williams, K.J. (2016) 'Gender variance in children and adolescents with autism spectrum disorder from the national database for autism research.' *International Journal of Transgenderism*, published online October 19, 2016: http://dx.doi.org/10.1080/15532739.2016.1241976.

McGuire, J.K. and Conover-Williams, M. (2010) 'Creating spaces to support transgender youth.' *The Prevention Researcher 17*, 4, 17–20.

McManama O'Brien, K.H., Putney, J.M., Hebert, N.W., Falk, A.M. and Aguinaldo, L.D. (2016) 'Sexual and gender minority youth suicide: Understanding subgroup differences to inform interventions.' *LGBT Health 3*, 4, 248–251.

Meier, S.L.C., Fitzgerald, K.M., Pardo, S.T. and Babcock, J. (2011) 'The effects of hormonal gender affirmation treatment on mental health in female-to-male transsexuals.' *Journal of Gay and Lesbian Mental Health 15*, 3, 281–299.

Meier, S.C. and Labuski, C.M. (2013) 'The Demographics of the Transgender Population.' In A.K. Baumle (ed.) *International Handbook on the Demography of Sexuality, International Handbooks of Population 5*. Dordrecht: Springer Science+Business Media.

Menvielle, E.J. and Hill, D.B. (2010) 'An affirmative intervention for families with gender-variant children: A process evaluation.' *Journal of Gay and Lesbian Mental Health 15*, 1, 94–123.

Menvielle, E.J. and Tuerk, C. (2002) 'A support group for parents of gender-nonconforming boys.' *Journal of the American Academy of Child and Adolescent Psychiatry 41*, 8, 1010–1013.

Menvielle, E.J., Tuerk, C. and Perrin, E.C. (2005) 'To the beat of a different drummer: The gender-variant child.' *Contemporary Pediatrics 22*, 12, 38–46.

Meyer, I.H. (2003) 'Prejudice, social stress, and mental health in lesbian, gay and bisexual populations: Conceptual issues and research evidence.' *Psychological Bulletin 129*, 5, 674–697.

Meyer, III, W., Bockting, W., Cohen-Kettinis, P., Coleman, E. *et al.* (2005) *The Standards of Care for Gender Identity Disorders* (Sixth Version). Minneapolis, MN: Harry Benjamin International Gender Dysphoria Association.

Milrod, C. (2014) 'How young is too young: Ethical concerns in genital surgery of the transgender MTF adolescent.' *Journal of Sexual Medicine 11*, 2, 338–346.

Mock, J. (2014) *Redefining Realness: My Path to Womanhood, Identity, Love and So Much More.* New York, NY: Atria Books.

Mock, J. (2017) 'The right to use the restroom.' *The New York Times*, February 26, 2017.

National Center for Transgender Equality (2016) *The Report of the 2015 U.S. Transgender Survey: Executive Summary.* Accessed on 3/1/17 at www.transequality.org/sites/default/files/docs/USTS-Executive-Summary-FINAL.PDF.

National Clearinghouse on Families and Youth (2016a) *Catering to Transgender Youths' Needs Supports Their Mental Health and Well-Being.* Accessed on 3/1/17 at http://ncfy.acf.hhs.gov/features/ncfy-reports-serving-transgender-youth/mental-health-wellbeing.

National Clearinghouse on Families and Youth (2016b) *From Foster Club: Tristan's Story.* Accessed on 3/1/17 at http://ncfy.acf.hhs.gov/features/ncfy-reports-serving-transgender-youth/tristans-story.

National Clearinghouse on Families and Youth (2016c) *Sexual Health and Transgender Youth.* Accessed on 3/1/17 at http://ncfy.acf.hhs.gov/features/ncfy-reports-serving-transgender-youth/sexual-health.

National Health Service (2014) *Disorder of Sex Development.* Accessed on 3/1/17 at www.nhs.uk/conditions/disorders-sex-development/Pages/Introduction.aspx.

NCCA Office of Inclusion (2011) NCAA Inclusion of Transgender Student-Athletes. Accessed on 3/19/2017 at www.transathlete.com/policies-college.

Nutt, A.E. (2015) *Becoming Nicole: The Transformation of an American Family.* New York, NY: Random House.

Ochs, R. and Rowley, S. (eds) (2005) *Getting Bi: Voices of Bisexuals Around the World.* Boston, MA: Bisexual Resource Center.

Olson, J., Forbes, C. and Belzer, M. (2011) 'Management of the transgender adolescent.' *Archives of Pediatric Adolescent Medicine 165*, 2, 171–176.

Olson-Kennedy, J., Rosenthal, S.M., Hastings, J. and Wesp, L. (2016) *Health Considerations for Gender Non-Conforming Children and Transgender Adolescents.* San Francisco, CA: Center of Excellence for Transgender Health, University of California. Accessed on 3/1/17 at http://transhealth.ucsf.edu/trans?page=guidelines-youth.

Paakkonen, Z.M. (2012) 'Legal Protections for Transgender Youth.' In J.L. Levi and E.E. Monnin-Browder (eds) *Transgender Family Law: A Guide to Effective Practice.* Bloomington, IN: Author House.

Perrotti, J. (2014) 'Partnering with Your Student's School.' Presentation at the GeMS Family Conference at Boston Children's Hospital. March 29, 2014.

Pleak, R. (2009) 'Formation of transgender identities in adolescence.' *Journal of Gay and Lesbian Mental Health 13*, 4, 282–291.

Reed, B.W.D., Cohen-Kettenis, P.T., Reed, T. and Spack, N. (2008) *Medical Care for Gender Variant Young People: Dealing with the Practical Problems*. Ashtead, Surrey, England: The Gender Identity Research and Education Society.

Reynolds, H.M. and Goldstein, Z.G. (2014) 'Social Transition.' In L. Erickson-Schroth (ed.) *Trans Bodies, Trans Selves*. New York, NY: Oxford University Press.

Riley, E.A., Sitharthan, G., Clemson, L. and Diamond, M. (2011) 'The needs of gender-variant children and their parents: A parent survey.' *International Journal of Sexual Health 23*, 3, 181–195.

Roosevelt, E. (1960) *You Learn by Living: Eleven Keys for a More Fulfilling Life*. Philadelphia, PA: The Westminster Press.

Rosenthal, S.M. (2014) 'Approach to the patient: Transgender youth: Endocrine considerations.' *Journal of Clinical Endocrinology and Metabolism 99*, 12, 4379–4389.

Russell, S.T. (2010) 'Contraindications and complexities in the lives of lesbian, gay, bisexual and transgender youth.' *The Prevention Researcher 17*, 4, 3–6.

Ryan, C. (2009) *Supportive Families, Healthy Children: Helping Families with Lesbian, Gay, Bisexual and Transgender Children*. San Francisco, CA: Family Acceptance Project, San Francisco State University.

Ryan, C. (2010) 'Engaging families to support lesbian, gay, bisexual and transgender youth.' *The Prevention Researcher 17*, 4, 11–13.

Schneider, M.S., Bockting, W.O., Ehrbar, R.D., Lawrence, A.A., Rachlin, K. and Zucker, K.J. (2009) *Report of the APA Task Force on Gender Identity and Gender Variance*. Washington, D.C.: American Psychological Association.

Serano, J. (2007) *Whipping Girl: A Transsexual Woman on Sexism and the Scapegoating of Femininity*. Berkeley, CA: Seal Press.

Serano, J. (2016) *Detransition, Desistance, and Disinformation: A Guide for Understanding Transgender Children Debates*. Accessed on 3/1/17 at https://medium.com/@juliaserano/detransition-desistance-and-disinformation-a-guide-for-understanding-transgender-children-993b7342946e#.h7mlzvuyr.

Shumer, D., Reisner, S.L., Edwards-Leeper, L. and Tishelman, A. (2016) 'Evaluation of Asperger Syndrome in youth presenting to a gender dysphoria clinic.' *LGBT Health 3*, 5, 387–390.

Solomon, A. (2012) *Far From the Tree: Parents, Children, and the Search for Identity*. New York, NY: Scribner.

Spack, N.P., Edwards-Leeper, L., Feldman, H.A., Leibowitz, S. *et al.* (2012) 'Children and adolescents with gender identity disorder referred to a pediatric medical center.' *Pediatrics 129*, 418–425.

Steensma, T.D., Biemond, R., de Boer, F. and Cohen-Kettenis, P.T. (2011) 'Desisting and persisting gender dysphoria after childhood: A qualitative follow-up study.' *Clinical Child Psychology and Psychiatry 16*, 4, 499–516.

Steensma, T.D., McGuire, J.K., Kreukels, B.P.C., Beekman, A.J. and Cohen-Kettenis, P.T. (2013) 'Factors associated with desistence and persistence of childhood gender dysphoria: A quantitative follow-up study.' *Journal of the American Academy of Child and Adolescent Psychiatry 52*, 6, 582–590.

Sue, D.W., Capodilupo, C.M., Torino, G.C., Bucceri, J.M. *et al.* (2007) 'Racial microaggressions in everyday life: Implications for clinical practice.' *American Psychologist 62*, 4, 271–286.

Teich, N.M. (2012) *Transgender 101: A Simple Guide to a Complex Issue*. New York, NY: Columbia University Press.

Testa, R.J., Coolhart, D. and Peta, J. (2015) *The Gender Quest Workbook: A Guide for Teens and Young Adults Exploring Gender Identity*. Oakland, CA: Instant Help Books.

Testa, R.J., Habarth, J., Peta, J., Balsam, K. and Bockting, W. (2015) 'Development of the gender minority stress and resilience measure.' *Psychology of Sexual Orientation and Gender Diversity 2*, 1, 65–77.

Tishelman, A.C., Kaufman, R., Edwards-Leeper, L., Mandel, F., Shumer, D. and Spack, N. (2015) 'Serving transgender youth: Challenges, dilemmas, and clinical examples.' *Professional Psychology: Research and Practice 46*, 1, 37–45.

Tom Waddell Health Center (2013) *Tom Waddell Health Center Protocols for Hormonal Reassignment of Gender*. Accessed on 3/1/17 at www.sfdph.org/dph/comupg/oservices/medSvs/hlthCtrs/TransGendprotocols122006.pdf.

Toomey, R.B., Ryan, C., Díaz, R.M., Card, N.A. and Russell, S.T. (2010) 'Gender-nonconforming lesbian, gay, bisexual, and transgender youth: School victimization and young adult psychosocial adjustment.' *Developmental Psychology 46*, 6, 1580–1589.

Transgender Australia (May, 2015) *Changing ID*. Accessed on 3/1/17 at http://transitioningdownunder.com/post/119670197286/changing-id.

Travers, R., Bauer, G., Pyne, J., Bradley, K., Gale, L. and Papadimitriou, M. (2012) *Impacts of Strong Parental Support for Trans Youth: A Report Prepared for Children's Aid Society of Toronto and Delisle Youth Services*. Accessed on 3/1/17 at http://transpulseproject.ca/wp-content/uploads/2012/10/Impacts-of-Strong-Parental-Support-for-Trans-Youth-vFINAL.pdf.

US Department of Justice (May 13, 2016) *U.S. Departments of Justice and Education Release Joint Guidance to Help Schools Ensure the Civil Rights of Transgender Students*. Accessed on 3/1/17 at www.justice.gov/opa/pr/us-departments-justice-and-education-release-joint-guidance-help-schools-ensure-civil-rights.

Vanderburgh, R. (2001) 'From female to not-female.' *In the Family 6*, 3, 26–27.

Vanderburgh, R. (2009) 'Appropriate therapeutic care for families with pre-pubescent transgender/gender-dissonant children.' *Child and Adolescent Social Work 26*, 2, 135–154.

Wallien, M.S.C. and Cohen-Kettenis, P.T. (2008) 'Psychosexual outcome of gender dysphoric children.' *Journal of the American Academy of Child and Adolescent Psychiatry 47*, 12, 1413–1423.

Westervelt, E. (2015) *At Age 3 – Transitioning from Jack to Jackie*. Washington, DC: NPR. Accessed on 3/1/17 at www.npr.org/sections/ed/2015/07/04/419498242/at-age-3-transitioning-from-jack-to-jackie?utm_source=npr_newsletter&utm_medium=email&utm_content=20150712&utm_campaign=mostemailed&utm_term=nprnews.

Winters, K. (2008) *Gender Madness in American Psychiatry: Essays from the Struggle for Dignity*. Dillon, CO: GID Reform Advocates.

Wu, J. and Broadus, K.W. (2012) 'Recognition of Name and Sex.' In J.L. Levi and J.L. Monnin-Browder (eds) *Transgender Family Law: A Guide to Effective Practice*. Bloomington, IN: Author House.

Subject Index

Author Index